PRAISE FOR
THE SEVEN WOUNDS OF CHRIST

"This is a powerful book of love, forgiveness and healing through Christ's wounds. In writing this book, Fred Hartley compels us to walk with Jesus, and each step allows us to look at Him differently. Each testimony reveals the awesomeness and power of our risen Lord. A riveting book, you won't want to put it down once you start reading."

—Jamel Patterson, MD

"Fred Hartley always glorifies Jesus in his writings. I've had the privilege of reading several of his books, and now comes this small book focusing on the powerful healing of our Lord and Savior, Jesus! I live in a land that needs healing—that needs Jesus. No one can heal like Jesus, for His healing is not just external, but also internal. The healing that Jesus gives empowers a person to then become healer to the wounded people around him or her. I recommend this book. The words you read will become part of your life and encourage you to be a man or woman of healing to others."

—Jack Sara
President, Bethlehem Bible College

"Fred Hartley forces us to examine the wounds of our Savior, knowing that as we face Jesus' unimaginable pain we also find His unimaginable love. *The Seven Wounds of Christ* takes us to the very depths of Christ's suffering so that we can more fully encounter the heights of His provision. 'By His wounds we are healed.'"

—Mike Scales
President, Nyack College

"As a history buff, I always enjoy making connections between times past and current events. *The Seven Wounds of Christ* is right up my alley. Fred Hartley does a masterful and meaningful job of recounting the immense suffering that Jesus experienced in His final hours and connects it to our suffering today. From a modern medical standpoint and as related to real-life experiences of people, Hartley shows proof positive to skeptics and cynics that there is a logical connection to Jesus' wounds. This is a powerfully moving book about the ultimate connectivity between suffering and forgiveness."

—Bob Van Rensselaer
Esquire, Attorney at Law

THE SEVEN WOUNDS OF CHRIST

WHERE SKEPTICS, CYNICS AND SEEKERS FIND UNEXPECTED HEALING

THE
SEVEN
WOUNDS
OF
CHRIST

WHERE SKEPTICS, CYNICS
AND SEEKERS FIND
UNEXPECTED HEALING

FRED A. HARTLEY III

CLC
PUBLICATIONS

Fort Washington, PA 19034

The Seven Wounds of Christ
Published by CLC Publications

U.S.A.
P.O. Box 1449, Fort Washington, PA 19034

UNITED KINGDOM
CLC International (UK)
Unit 5, Glendale Avenue, Sandycroft, Flintshire, CH5 2QP

© 2017 Fred A. Hartley III
All rights reserved. Published 2017

Printed in the United States of America

ISBN (hardcover): 978-1-61958-258-3
ISBN (e-book): 978-1-61958-259-0

Italics in Scripture quotations are the emphasis of the author.

Cover design by Mitch Bolton.

DEDICATION

To my community of friends living in metro Atlanta,
born in sixty-five different nations of the world,
who have become my family—my home—
known as Lilburn Alliance Church.
You are a miracle!
I love and honor you for so many reasons.
You prove to me every day
by the marriages saved,
diseases healed,
addictions conquered,
identities restored,
guilt and shame removed,
self-hatred overcome,
family legacies recovered
and lives redeemed,
that there truly is healing
in the seven wounds of Christ.

CONTENTS

FOREWORD

For many years I have had the privilege of partnering with Fred Hartley in the College of Prayer International and facilitating prayer gatherings throughout the world. We have seen God move in miraculous and healing ways all across the globe. In the presence of Christ, the blind received their sight, the lame walked and the deaf heard. To the glory of God, prayer movements have begun in small villages and in the highest halls of government. And everywhere we have been, people have shared with us their deep wounds—wounds that have come from family, church and friends.

Fred takes you to the only place where your wounds can be healed. I believe that our wounded healer, the Lord Jesus Christ, wants to use this book to transform your wounds into triumphs, redeem your pain and keep you from wasting your sorrows. The key to your healing is your union with Christ. Fred lays out the vital connection between the wounds of Jesus and the healing power He has made available for your wounds. The Holy Spirit makes the things of Jesus real to you. The Spirit's work is to smite you with the beauty of Jesus and bring forth beauty from your ashes. When you come to the Lord for healing, more often than not, the Holy Spirit brings up painful memories from your past. Memories hold on to the pain of wounds. While grieving your wounds is always helpful, nothing is more powerful than inviting the healing presence of Jesus into the memories and into the pain.

I was at a large youth conference when a teenage girl came to me for ministry. The young woman had responded to the gospel by giving her life to Christ, and her friends were so excited for her. However, the next day, as she reacted to a message about the empowerment of the Holy Spirit for godly living and Christian service, she began to lose control of herself. She started experiencing strange physical manifestations and the emotional reactions of a person who had been abused, so she came to me for help. When I saw this young woman for the first time, it struck me how pale and withdrawn she looked. Her eyes were lifeless. She would not look at anyone directly and seemed to be trying to disappear. I found out that she was around fifteen years old and that during her sophomore year of high school she had been gang raped. The pain and fear of that terrible violation had come flooding back to her as she attempted to yield her life to the fullness of the Holy Spirit. She sat before me broken and afraid.

There are no words to speak to such a wound, no pat answers. I asked her if we could invite Jesus into her wounds, into her pain. She said yes. We began to pray and seek the Lord together. She willingly opened up the memory of the rape again, only this time allowing Jesus to minister to her pain. I watched her as I prayed with her. Her forehead clearly indicated by its movement that she was reliving that awful event. She shared with me that she was not alone but that Jesus had taken her into His arms and was wiping away her tears. Her memory and her wounds would never be the same. She would never have to remember that violation of her person without seeing Jesus there, protecting and embracing her.

I asked if she had heard Him say anything else. She said, "Yes. He is asking me to forgive those who did this to me." One by one, one name at a time, she forgave the rapists out loud with me. I knew that she would have to forgive them for her own healing and freedom, but I had not asked her to do so. Jesus asked her, and she did it. When she opened her eyes, she was not the same person. Jesus had given her, in only a few moments, a substantial healing. Her eyes were bright and shiny. She held her head erect and was able to look me right in the eye with dignity and freedom. The Holy Spirit had made the healing of Jesus real to her, and she was smitten with His beauty.

Press into this book. Make the exchange—your pain for His healing. Let the Spirit of God smite your heart with the beauty of Jesus. Jesus is more real than your pain.

Dr. Mike Plunket
Professor, Nyack College,
Alliance Theological Seminary
Lead Pastor, Risen King Alliance Church

PREFACE

Ground Zero: The point on the earth's surface above and below an exploding nuclear bomb. The central point in an idea of fast change or intense activity.

The cross of Christ marks ground zero for all humankind throughout human history. When Jesus walked down the Via Dolorosa, the path of pain, to the place of His crucifixion, His sufferings formed a nuclear explosion of epic proportions and impacted everything above the cross and beneath it—both the justice and mercy of God above and the desperate wounds of humanity below. In this book, we will journey along the places where Christ's seven wounds occurred, and we will discover the explosive work of Christ that does not destroy but rather heals wounded, brutalized people. The combined wounds of Christ form the central point of redemption that brings the fastest life change and most intense healing activity anywhere on the planet.

This week, as I finish editing this book, I am in Jerusalem of all places. While walking the streets of the Old City, I have realized something I never noticed in my earlier trips here: cynics, skeptics and seekers are all here, gathering around Christ's wounds. And as we walk through this book, you and I will be among them. Throughout these pages, we will walk together down the street known as the Via Dolorosa, the path of pain.

Let's face it—we are bruised and bleeding people. Though our wounds have come to us in ruthless and unexpected ways—whether financial, emotional, marital, moral or physical—we have each walked our own path of pain and have our own ways of dealing with suffering. Some of us pick our scabs obsessively only to make them bleed again, while others of us try to look the other way in denial. As C.S. Lewis wisely wrote, "Pain insists upon being attended to. God whispers to us in our pleasures, speaks in our conscience, but shouts in our pain: it is his megaphone to rouse a deaf world."[1] Sooner or later we need to face the music, no matter how bad the music sounds. Wounds require attention.

It is always easier to face our wounds when we know there is a cure. The wounds of Jesus do just that. Jesus' wounds are not for religious people but for wounded people. There is nothing religious about the cross. Jesus was not crucified in a church between two candelabras; He was nailed to a cross that stood between two thieves. For this reason, this book is not so much for religious people but for people willing to face their wounds. The words of the Hebrew prophet Isaiah explain well the truth that Jesus' wounds were meant to heal ours: "Surely he took up our pain / and bore our suffering. . . . He was pierced for our transgressions, / he was crushed for our iniquities."[2] Jesus' wounds are our wounds, and His wounds are for our healing. Somehow as we walk the Via Dolorosa, our paths of pain converge with His path of pain. But let's not get ahead of ourselves! We will discover our healing as we move forward one step and one wound at a time.

Make no mistake about it—the cross is a scandal! Even the first-century preacher Paul said that he preached of "Christ crucified, a stumbling block [skandalon]."[3] A skandalon was a moveable stick that served as a trigger in a trap. It was like a hidden and bent sapling used to catch prey. Those of us who have ever felt ripped off, cheated and scandalized in life will discover that we have a friend in Jesus who was more scandalized than any of us could imagine. No matter how deep our wounds or how acute our pain, the wounds of Jesus go deeper.

This book will take us on a step-by-step journey along the Via Dolorosa, where we will investigate each of Jesus' seven wounds at the places where He received them. We will begin our discussion of each wound with a medical explanation of what Jesus experienced. Yes, a down-to-earth scientific explanation. We want to initially understand Jesus as the man of the first century in order to maintain the objectivity of our study.

Each chapter contains three parts. The first is titled Christ's Surrender. Too often we bundle the wounds of Christ together in a single unjust violent incident and thereby miss the fuller impact of His suffering. In reality, each of Jesus' wounds corresponds to a separate voluntary choice of surrender by Christ. He willingly submitted Himself to seven distinct experiences of extraordinary pain, each one for a distinctive redemptive purpose.

The second part is Our Healing. Every wound of Christ corresponds to a wound in you and in me. While all seven of Christ's wounds reflect the completeness of His atonement, looking at each one individually will help us appreciate what Jesus did for us and also appropriate it.

We will end each chapter with the final part, A Twenty-First-Century Healing. This section will provide an honest and accurate real-life story to illustrate how Jesus' wounds bring healing today. In the last book of the Bible, we are told of followers of Jesus who "triumphed over [the devil] / by the blood of the Lamb / and by the word of their testimony; / they did not love their lives so much / as to shrink from death."[4] All eight of these real-life stories dramatically illustrate that Jesus' wounds offer us healing as well as victory. God wants to heal us, and He also wants us to be overcomers.

A person could certainly read *The Seven Wounds of Christ* in a single sitting—it should take less time than watching a full-length movie. I recommend, however, reading this book in just over a week, a single chapter each day. Take your time. Chew on it. Let it soak in. Don't just read it—think! If you are in a small group and want to use the book for a stimulating eight-week study, group application questions are included at the end of the book for your convenience.

My deepest appreciation in writing this book goes to my greatest treasure and inspiration, my wife, Sherry; to my loyal and efficient administrative assistant, Heather Hatcher; to my proofreader, Ann Miller, and editor, Becky English; to my Managing Editor, Erika Cobb, who walked with me through thick and thin; to my contributing historic and biblical experts Josh Smith and Bill Hyer; to my medical science experts Dr. Art Nitz, MD, (PhD, faculty professor of Physical Therapy for thirty years at the University of Kentucky) and Stephen Trinidad (fourth-year honor student at Icahn School of Medicine at Mount Sinai in New York City); and to Cesar Castellanos for his pastor's heart and inspiring book *Victory Through the Blood*, elevating the benefits of each of Christ's wounds. And finally, I am indebted to Christ and His good people at Lilburn Alliance Church, who demonstrate to me every day that there truly is healing in the seven wounds of Christ.

Getting to write this book is unquestionably one of the greatest privileges of my life. It has made me feel less like a scholar and more like the donkey that carried Jesus into Jerusalem. While I did my best to effectively communicate the potency of His wounds, my role is virtually nothing compared to what Christ endured to receive them.

1

WALK WITH ME!
His Wounds, Our Healing

When the soldiers had crucified Jesus, they took his garments and divided them into four parts, one part for each soldier; also his tunic. But the tunic was seamless, woven in one piece from top to bottom, so they said to one another, "Let us not tear it, but cast lots for it to see whose it shall be."

John 19: 23–24

The Via Dolorosa is a narrow, well-worn street that cuts through the Old City of Jerusalem like a scar on a cheek. This unassuming road starts in the garden of Gethsemane at the base of the Mount of Olives, enters the Old City at the Lion's Gate, and proceeds through the Muslim Quarter into the Christian Quarter until it reaches the Church of the Holy

Sepulcher. It is arguably the most visited street in the world even though it measures only a thousand meters, or approximately 3,280 feet.

Via Dolorosa is Latin for "way of grief," "way of sorrow" or "way of suffering"—or simply, as we will call it, "the path of pain." The path is marked by nine stations of the cross; there are five additional stations inside the Church of the Holy Sepulcher.[1]

On this path of pain, Jesus received His seven wounds.

Let's take a walk. The Old City of Jerusalem is buzzing with activity. Street vendors wheel out their racks of prayer shawls, T-shirts and water pipes, while others hand squeeze delicious pomegranate juice. A moped whizzes by. Everyone is getting ready for a big day. The air is crisp, the aroma of freshly grilled shawarma awakens people's appetites, and the atmosphere pulsates with a strong cadence of vitality. It's going to be another pristine day in the Old City. There is no city on earth like Jerusalem.

Our hike normally takes thirty minutes at walking speed—a little more than a thousand steps —but today we will spend several hours along the path of pain. Our objective is not simply to get from point A to point B in record time but to familiarize ourselves with the historical places where Jesus' wounds occurred and to pause at strategic sites. We want to learn what we can about

Jesus and His seven wounds—and face some of our own wounds along the way.

THE HILL OF THE SKULL

We start our walk at the scene of Jesus' crucifixion: Golgotha, known as "the hill of the skull," where the Church of the Holy Sepulcher now stands. This is actually where the Via Dolorosa ends, but because in many ways it is ground zero, it is only appropriate for us to begin our overview of Jesus' path of suffering here.

Formal church buildings have always made me feel awkward. The Church of the Holy Sepulcher in the Old City of Jerusalem would be no exception, except for one thing: This is the exact location where most scholars and historians tell us Jesus was crucified. It sits just outside the original wall around the Holy City. It is where criminals were taken to be executed.

Inside the church, I am jostled by a throng of people from virtually every nation on earth waiting to see the precise historic stones where Jesus was crucified. As I inch ever closer, fighting to maintain my place in line, I am initially hit with the overkill of religious symbols— the gaudy velour drapes and tacky candelabras that make the scene look less like a historical shrine and more like the lighting department at Home Depot. But then I see what I had been hoping for—my eyes lock on the ancient stones that mark the place where the cross of Jesus stood. Much to my delight, I discover that a sizable outcropping of limestone has been preserved under a large plate of protective Plexiglas. This spot marks the place where the majority of Jesus' blood was poured.

Some around me kneel. Many weep. Both men and women stare with laser-like focus, riveted on the rocks over which He died. People are respectful, even reverent. Some take pictures, but the moment is too weighty, too profound for anyone to cheapen it with a selfie. Everyone seems to have the same sense: This is more about Jesus than anyone or anything else. I have been to this exact spot a dozen times before, but I never felt what I feel today. Having spent the previous twelve months extensively researching the seven wounds of Christ, I am overwhelmed with unexpected emotion as I realize that my passion, my suffering, is viscerally linked to Christ's. It is as if I am the only one standing here. I feel connected with God on an unusually deep level—spiritually, intellectually and emotionally. From the moment my eyes see the rock, all the historic significance of the grotesque mangling and physical abuse Jesus suffered seem to simultaneously draw my heart to God. I sigh. My arms fall limp to my sides. My mouth drops open.

As I stand gazing, I am overwhelmed by the realization that the seven wounds in Jesus' body from which He bled are as equally accessible to you and me today as they were to His followers two thousand years ago. I exhale slowly in profound gratitude. I shake my head and cry out loud, "My God, my God, how much You must love me to subject Your Son to such hostility. And to think that You did it for me—for all of us!"

In one way or another, the goal of this short book is to give you, too, a similar moment of profound and even breathtaking appreciation of the seven wounds of Christ. I will do my best to accurately stick with the facts we know from historical documents; thankfully, the final hours before Jesus' dead body was laid in the tomb have been meticulously recorded. You, however, can reach your own conclusions. Whether you are a skeptic, cynic or seeker, I respect your perspective and invite you to think objectively about the death of Jesus, whom many call the Christ, the Anointed, the Messiah.

Though I have many times walked past the historic stones of Golgotha, something new hits me this time. Standing around me are Japanese, Filipinos, Brazilians, Europeans, Arabs, Nigerians, Christians, Jews and even Muslims, each one elbowing their way ever closer to the precise stones on which two thousand years ago the blood of Jesus was poured out. The mass of seekers press uncomfortably close together, barely capable of containing their eagerness to get a firsthand eyewitness look at these historic stones.

I realize that we are staring at more than archeological ruins. As a historian, I have visited ancient stones and archeological digs in countless other locations, but none of them have generated this level of electricity. What makes these stones so supercharged is that all of us who are observing them share one thing in common: We are all wounded people looking for healing. Toward the end of our journey, we will return here to these stones to take a closer look, but for now we must move on.

THE WHIPPING STONE

A mere one hundred meters from the place of Jesus' execution is a little-known excavation site forty-five feet underground. We turn left down a narrow unmarked alley and trek down three flights of stairs to see a Roman whipping stone, only recently discovered. Most pilgrims walk right past the stairway and miss this gem.

Roman whipping stone

Huddled together in the dimly lit stone chamber, we stand around an ancient Roman whipping stone that rises in the middle of the chamber and dates back two thousand years. Here criminals were tied and brutally beaten with the flagellum. Off to the side, chiseled in the stone floor, a dice game resembling a chess or backgammon board shows where soldiers gambled. "While it is impossible to guarantee with 100 percent accuracy that this is the exact location where Jesus was ruthlessly beaten prior to crucifixion," our antiquities expert explains, "it is certainly likely. It is strikingly similar to the way the ancient documents describe the beating of Christ, with both its whipping stone and its game board where soldiers gambled for Jesus' robe." The voice of our tour guide echoes through the all-stone enclosed room as he reads the penetrating words of Isaiah, the ancient Hebrew prophet.

> *Surely he has borne our griefs*
>   *and carried our sorrows;*
> *yet we esteemed him stricken,*
>   *smitten by God, and afflicted.*
> *But he was pierced for our transgressions;*
>   *he was crushed for our iniquities;*
> *upon him was the chastisement that brought us peace,*
>   *and with his wounds we are healed.*
> *All we like sheep have gone astray;*
>   *we have turned—every one—to his own way;*
> *and the* LORD *has laid on him*
>   *the iniquity of us all.*[2]

Every word echoes in the stone chamber where we stand—and deep within our souls. The single word that stands out to me is "our"—our griefs, our sorrows, our transgressions, our iniquities. All of a sudden it hits me— Jesus did it all for us! His wounds were for our wounds. Then I am hit with the words "with his wounds we are healed." Really? I think to myself. Do Christ's wounds somehow carry a miraculous power still potent enough to pack a healing wallop today—for my precious daughter, Andrea, who is right now battling stage IV cancer?

After a full minute of silence, our teacher suggests, "I want you to think for a moment right now about the wounds in your own life, in the lives of family members, friends, loved ones. Take a minute or two in isolation before you leave this place, and think about your wounds. Take this opportunity to confront your own woundedness, fears and insecurities. Remember—with His wounds we are healed."

I am overwhelmed with emotion. Once again I feel as if I am the only one present. Tears roll down my cheeks as I hold my wife's hand. We lock eyes, and I notice that she too is crying as we think of our daughter in Dallas battling inoperable large B-cell lymphoma that has wrapped itself around the major blood vessels surrounding her heart. Lord, is there healing here today for our precious daughter, Andrea? Will You extend healing to her?

Having studied the seven wounds of Christ for the past year, my mind easily recalls each one, and I think deeply: If He was pierced for our transgressions, this must mean that He was pierced for my transgressions too. If He was crushed for our iniquities, my iniquities must have been included. If the chastisement that brought us peace was upon Him, that means it can bring me peace as well, right? If by His wounds, we are healed, could that mean that my precious daughter, Andrea, is included?

As I look around at the others in the chamber, it is obvious that Sherry and I are not the only ones crying. Tears moisten virtually every face. It makes perfect sense. Every tear is linked to a very real and personal heart wound—emotional, moral, spiritual, marital, financial. George has just lost his job and is battling the wound of self-worth. He is terrified about his future. Sharita was divorced last year and, as a single mom, is fighting a spirit of rejection and loneliness. Helen recently acknowledged that she was sexually abused as a child and has spent most of her adult life battling guilt, shame and sexual brokenness. All at once, I understand why millions of people every year, from virtually every nation on earth, flock to Israel—and specifically to the Via Dolorosa, the place of Christ's pain and suffering. We are all wounded people visiting the sites of Jesus' wounds.

In a real way, Jesus' wounds are our wounds. It is impossible to accurately consider the historic wounds of Jesus without fully recognizing and embracing our own wounds. Not only are Jesus' wounds our wounds, but Jesus' wounds are our healing. Isaiah was clear when he prophesied that our healing would come from the wounds of Christ. Jesus was wounded for us! When we think of His wounds, we do not just sympathize with them or rejoice that He sympathizes with ours; rather we encounter our healing within His wounds. Jesus was wounded that His wounds might heal ours.

Acknowledging His woundedness goes hand in hand with acknowledging ours. This short book is as much about self-discovery as historic discovery. It takes us on a trip back two thousand years in time, and at the same time it takes us on a trip deep within our own souls. Without a trip to both locations, reading this book would be a waste of time. As we examine the seven wounds of Christ, the wounds will examine us. They have a way of getting under one's skin. Before we know what has happened, Christ's wounds will lead us to the profound reality that God wants to get beneath the surface of our lives. Many people struggle with denial when it comes to facing personal brokenness, inner woundedness and emotional pain because they feel hopeless. If we look only at our wounds, we will be hopeless. If we look to Christ's wounds, however, our hopelessness will begin to fade, and the hope of healing will start to rise. This is why the gospel of Christ is called the good news. The wounds of Jesus may convert you to hope, and hope is the doorway to your healing.

THE GARDEN OF GETHSEMANE

We leave the underground chamber of the whipping stone, and after a twenty-minute walk, we come to the garden where Jesus received His first wound. Gethsemane, a place Jesus loved and where the Via Dolorosa actually begins, is one of the only sites along the path of pain whose original natural beauty has been preserved.

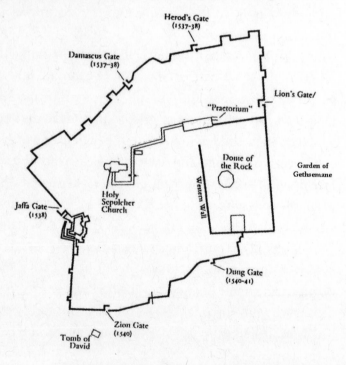

The Via Dolorosa in modern-day Jerusalem

Many of the olive trees that stand today, with massive trunks nearly fifteen feet in circumference, are in fact two thousand years old. Here in the garden, Jesus processed many of His life-changing moments, and this beautiful place also provides us with a chance to reflect on what we've already seen and to prepare for what is to come.

As we walk through this book, I have three suggestions. *Have hope.* Without hope it is impossible for us to face our wounds. We tend to run and hide from our wounds and weaknesses, but there is nothing more hopeful than knowing that there is a God who loves us so much that He has already sent His Son to be wounded with our wounds.

Get real. There is nothing on earth more raw, real and naked than the cross where Jesus died. He had nothing to hide, and He held nothing back. If we want to meet Him at the cross, He expects as much from us. The best definition of humility I ever heard is this: Humility is the willingness to be known for who we are. No mask. No cover-up. No pretense. Just come as we are, wounds and all. When Christ received our wounds, He already made a public spectacle of our sin and shame. He already let the cat out of the bag, so we no longer need to hide.

Go deep. There is no way Jesus allowed the metal stakes to be driven through His wrists and ankles and the spear to be thrust into His side, only to have a superficial relationship with us. If the cross tells us anything, it is that God wants to go deep. Just as Jesus' wounds went deep into Him, He wants His healing to go deep into us. The fact that Jesus was wounded is historically irrefutable. By the grace of God, before the end of this book, we will fully understand that it is equally irrefutable that His seven wounds can bring healing to us today.

A TWENTY-FIRST-CENTURY SEEKER

Michael was a wounded man with a wounded heart. He felt condemned and filled with shame. He is the first of eight wounded people we will be introduced to throughout this book. Although he lived in the Old City of Jerusalem—the crossroads of the religious traditions of Judaism, Christianity and Islam—and had grown up hearing arguments for each of these major religions, he felt lost. Not knowing where to turn and with a sense of deep desperation, he came to the Church of the Sepulcher. It was the same night, of all nights, that my team and I just happened to be walking the streets of the Old City with a purpose of our own—to talk to people about the love of Jesus.

Michael told us, "I came here as a last ditch effort. I am so depressed that I want to die. Either Jesus will help me or . . ." He broke down. It was no coincidence that we were there to meet him. Even more significantly, it was at the exact place where Christ was wounded for him. Michael was seeking answers, and it's fair to say that God was seeking him. Two of our team members looked into Michael's eyes and felt his despair, loneliness and emptiness. Michael told them his story; and that night, as they stood within a few feet of the place where Christ was first wounded, they told Michael about the wounds of Christ and then led him in prayer. That night Michael encountered God's love for perhaps the first time in his life. He learned firsthand that the wounds of Christ are for our healing.

There is love in the wounds of Jesus. If you miss the love, you miss the point. Love is what led Jesus to the cross, and it's what initiated God's redemptive plan. Perhaps you've heard these words before: "For God so loved the world that he gave his one and only Son, that whoever believes in him shall not perish but have eternal life."[3] Again, God is not seeking a superficial relationship with you. He loves you. He wants to go deep with you—as deep as the wounds of Christ.

Now that we have gotten an overview of the Via Dolorosa and understand where we are going, it's time for our journey to begin. We'll start at the base of the Mount of Olives in the garden of Gethsemane, just outside the Old City.

2

THE SWEAT OF JESUS
Reshaping Our Wills

Being in agony he prayed more earnestly; and his sweat became like great drops of blood falling down to the ground.

Luke 22: 44

Hematidrosis is a medical term used to describe the explosion of capillaries surrounding the sweat glands. While this physiological phenomenon is not common, neither is it unknown. It happens under times of extreme stress and anxiety when the human body tries to sweat faster than it normally does, which causes the blood vessels around the sweat glands to burst, creating a reddish-pink color in every drop of perspiration. The microscopic skin tissue then explodes and excretes both blood and pigment.

Medical scientists have documented several cases of hematidrosis. A traumatized young girl who had extreme anxiety during war suffered hematidrosis when gas exploded in a house near her. On another occasion a Catholic nun who was threatened by sword-carrying soldiers suffered hematidrosis and bled from every part of her body. She eventually died of anxiety, hemorrhaging even though her assailants never touched her. More recently, at the end of the twentieth century, seventy-six cases of hematidrosis have been documented.

While the extent of blood loss with hematidrosis is normally minimal, its occurrence results in the skin being excessively tender, fragile and sensitive to touch or abrasions. This is likely what happened to Jesus in the garden of Gethsemane.

Our journey with Jesus down the path of pain starts in a garden. Picture an orchard of well-cared-for olive trees, where birds take nest and ground squirrels thrive. What would culminate fifteen hours after the start of Jesus' walk, in arguably the most inhumane act of injustice in human history, began in this innocuous and tranquil place, only a thousand meters from the site of His crucifixion.

This quiet getaway that Jesus loved is located at the base of the Mount of Olives. He often went to this secluded, peaceful place to clear His head, center Himself, and get His bearings before major decision-making moments. After celebrating an eventful Passover meal with His disciples, He left the upper room, walked a half-mile through the Kidron Valley, and entered this quiet, lovely garden known as Gethsemane.

Olive tree in garden of Gethsemane

The name "Gethsemane" literally means "olive press" and is derived from the Hebrew word *gatshamanim*. This garden served as an agricultural refinery for olive oil. First-century farmers harvested their olive trees and then carried their bags of fruit down the hillside to be processed in an olive press. Their fruit would then be crushed into useful oil—some as fluid for lamps and some as anointing oil. The ancient olive press was made of a very few but significant moving parts. There was the huge, solid stone base; the round crushing stone, weighing anywhere from several hundred to a thousand pounds; and the wood beam inserted in the center of the crushing stone that gave leverage to the person or animal moving the stone around the circumference of the base stone in order to crush the olives.

On Jesus' last night in the garden, however, the olive press of Gethsemane was not crushing olives. The heavy cylindrical crushing stone sat motionless. On this night, it was the will and resolve of Jesus that was being crushed. This process was not refining oil but refining His human spirit.

CHRIST'S SURRENDER

Every wound of Christ corresponds to an act of surrender of Christ's will. After all, Jesus explicitly said to His disciples, "I lay down my life that I may take it up again. No one takes it from me, but I lay it down of my own accord. I have authority to lay it down, and I have authority to take it up again. This charge I have received from my Father."[1] Jesus would later say specifically to His enemies who inflicted His wounds, "You would have no authority over me at all unless it had been given you from above,"[2] and, "Do you think that I cannot appeal to my Father, and he will at once send me more than twelve legions of angels?"[3] With this first wound, Jesus submitted His will to be crushed, like a ripe, plump olive, between a rock and a hard place.

It is significant that the crushing of Jesus' will took place in prayer: "My Father, if this cup cannot pass unless I drink it, your will be done."[4] Again He prayed, "Father, if you are willing, remove this cup from me. Nevertheless, not my will, but yours, be done."[5] Notice how often in this short prayer Jesus referred to the will—no less than four times! The will was the issue. Like an athlete or warrior, He did not want to miss His moment. Jesus had spent every day of His thirty-three years on earth intentionally yielding to the will of His Father, God. Now He wanted to finish the race and fulfill His life's purpose. The historic account provides us with a graphic description of the intensity of Jesus' battle: "Being in agony he prayed more earnestly; and his sweat became like great drops of blood falling down to the ground."[6] Notice the blood. This is the first mention of drops of blood from Jesus' body. The battle Jesus fought in the garden was to subjugate His own will to the will of His Father, and this struggle caused the first of His seven wounds as He sweat drops of blood.

Some skeptics have argued against the accuracy or even the possibility of this account. They argue that the early Gospel writers were trying too hard to dramatize the intensity of Christ's struggle. In their effort to be scientifically objective, however, they overlooked the scientific explanation of what we now know to be hematidrosis.

The larger question that must be raised is: Why was Jesus under such intense stress in the first place? Why were His sweat glands exploding and His perspiration full of blood pigmentation? The anticipation of the physical torment He would endure over the next fifteen hours certainly accounts for part of His extreme anxiety, but that is only a partial answer. The weightier reason for His anguish is that, against all odds, He chose to surrender His will to the unthinkable: to take all the wounds of all humanity throughout all history into His own body. The thought of all disease, dysfunction, self-hatred, anxiety, addiction, pride, lust, arrogance, violence and injustice being injected into His system was so horrific that He understandably bled from virtually every pore in His body.

Just as Jesus surrendered His will, He would also surrender, in each of His successive wounds, His personal identity, His physical health, His dignity, His productivity and His authority. Most excruciating of all, He would surrender His intimacy and relational heart union with God. This first wound of Jesus' was not inflicted by a person—it was exacted upon Him by His realization of all He would face by noon the next day. This wound set in motion all the other wounds. In the final hours of His life, Jesus would bleed from seven different places, and His journey started with hematidrosis.

Here in the olive press of Gethsemane, the will of Jesus was crushed into oil—much like the anointing oil. The distinct name "Christ" means "Messiah," or "anointed one." The ancient Jewish Scriptures promised that an anointed one would yet come and would one day announce, "The Spirit of the Lord GOD is upon me, / because the LORD has anointed me / to bring good news to the poor; / he has sent me to bind up the brokenhearted, / to proclaim liberty to the captives, / and the opening of the prison to those who are bound."[7]

This same Jesus who prayed His prayer of surrender in the garden of Gethsemane had three years earlier taken the scroll of Isaiah in the synagogue in Nazareth and read these identical words. Then, after reading the passage, he sat down on Moses' seat in the synagogue in Nazareth and announced, much to the shock and awe of His Jewish audience, "Today this Scripture has been fulfilled in your hearing."[8] It is impossible to miss the fact that Jesus, who claimed to be the promised Anointed One, was being crushed like olives in the olive press of Gethsemane as anointing oil.

As we think of straining every nerve and expending every drop of energy, world-class athlete Michael Phelps comes to mind. As the most decorated Olympian of all time, it is easy to see him standing on top of the medal stand receiving his awards. We can hear his national anthem playing in the background as he exudes exuberant pride. What few people stop to consider are the countless hours of conditioning Phelps put in prior to his world-class achievements, which made him arguably the greatest Olympic athlete of all time. Before he set his thirty-four world records and earned his twenty-eight Olympic medals— including twenty-three gold, with fifteen more medals than any other swimmer in history, and earning the most gold medals in individual events (thirteen), and the most gold medals in a single year (eight in Beijing in 2008)—he worked like a dog when no one was watching. Before he went to his first Olympic games, at only fifteen years of age, he would wake up in the dark and head to the swimming pool while most kids his age were still sound asleep. In his peak training days, he would work five to seven hours a day, six days a week— swimming a minimum of 80,000 meters, or a whopping fifty miles, each week![9] And that just accounts for what he did inside the swimming pool. In addition, he did extensive weight training including squats, push-ups, pull-ups, dead lifts, bench presses and more. And he did all of this when no one was watching. Because of his rigorous conditioning, his heart pumped double the amount of blood as the average adult male. When Michael showed up in Rio for his fifth Olympic appearance, he knew he was competing against swimmers almost half his age. Many sports analysts questioned his fitness, but Michael trusted his training and left nothing in his tank. As impressive as Michael Phelps' workout is, Christ exerted even more mental toughness in the garden of Gethsemane. His resolve and determination were pushed beyond normal human limits. To my knowledge, Phelps never sweated drops of blood. What Phelps did in the swimming pool when no one was watching is a reflection of what Christ did in the garden. As excruciating as it was for Him in the garden, His sufferings prepared Him for the battle that was yet to come.

It should not be surprising that the only one of the four Gospel writers to include the medical account of hematidrosis was the only medical doctor in the group—Dr. Luke.

OUR HEALING

This first wound of Jesus corresponds to the first wound of humankind—the wound to our wills. This wound dates all the way back to another garden—the garden of Eden. It was in Eden that Adam and Eve, the first two representatives of humankind, were created by a loving Father God and given open access to His manifest presence. They walked with God in the cool of the day and enjoyed intimacy with their creator. To protect the intimacy of their loving relationship with Him, they were given limited yet specific guidelines: "You may surely eat of every tree of the garden, but of the tree of the knowledge of good and evil you shall not eat, for in the day that you eat of it you shall surely die."[10] Before long, however, they intentionally violated their love parameters and chose to disobey. This corruption of will twisted and wounded the genetics of their internal disposition toward God, and the result proved catastrophic. Because of Adam and Eve's rebellion, we are all now wounded, broken people. Our wills all too often lead us to make boneheaded, self-destructive, addiction-forming, self-loathing decisions. Martin Luther, the great Christian Reformer, had it right in his book *The Bondage of the Will*, in which he explained how the will has been in bondage to evil ever since the willful disobedience of Adam and Eve in the garden. Even the apostle Paul candidly wrote, "I do not do what I want, but I do the very thing I hate."[11] Most honest people can identify with the reality of a wounded will.

It is no coincidence that the redemption work of Jesus started in a garden. In the garden of Gethsemane Jesus set in motion the entire plan of redemption by which He would reverse the curse that had been set in motion in the garden of Eden. If we are to believe the historical accuracy of the early biblical writers, in the first garden, Adam and Eve disobeyed; in the second garden, Christ obeyed. In Eden, Adam and Eve rejected the cup of blessing; in Gethsemane, Christ drank the cup of cursing. Adam and Eve wanted to be like God in Eden; in Gethsemane, Christ chose to be like us. The first two people displeased Father God in Eden; in Gethsemane, Christ pleased Father God. In a sense, the first people ruined everything in the garden of Eden; but in the garden of Gethsemane, Christ redeemed everything. Adam and Eve walked away from God's manifest presence in Eden; but in Gethsemane, Christ regained for us God's manifest presence. The serpent won in Eden, but the serpent lost in Gethsemane.

The mission of Jesus was to restore the blessings of the first garden, and He appropriately began that process in another garden.

Garden of Eden	Garden of Gethsemane
Humanity disobeyed	Christ obeyed
Humanity lost God's manifest presence	Christ restored God's manifest presence
Humanity rejected the cup of blessing	Christ drank the cup of cursing
Humanity wanted to be like God	Christ chose to be like us
Humanity displeased God	Christ pleased God
Humanity ruined everything	Christ redeemed everything
Serpent won	Serpent lost

The battle against good and evil is won or lost in the will. If Jesus is going to do anything of substance for us today, He must begin the process by affecting our wills. If He can change our wills, He can change us. The first step toward our redemption is to recognize that our wills are in trouble. If we can embrace the reality of our own twisted wills and motivations, we become candidates for Christ's healing.

The incredibly exciting news is this: Because Christ surrendered His will, He is able to redeem ours. As Michael Phelps endured excruciating conditioning to win the gold medals for his country, Christ endured excruciating testing in Gethsemane to win our healing and our redemption. For this reason, the Bible makes an audacious promise to us: "It is God who works in you, both to will and to work for his good pleasure."[12] Do yourself a favor and read these hopeful words again. God promises that He is able to change our wills so that we are now able to will God's will. He not only changes our wills, but He changes our ability to do His will, because He works in us "both to will and to work for his good pleasure."

This is the story of redemption, and it started in a garden. This is the miracle of the wound to Jesus' sweat glands. He surrendered His will in order to transform our wills and release them from bondage to the power of evil, making it possible for us to now obey God.

A TWENTY-FIRST-CENTURY HEALING

Jack became an angry teenager after he experienced harsh and unjust treatment by the Israelis. He grew up on, of all places, the Via Dolorosa in the Old City of Jerusalem. As a fourteen-year-old Arab youth living in Israel, he was often ruthlessly abused by Israeli soldiers, grabbed as an innocent pedestrian doing nothing but walking down the street, dragged into prison, blindfolded, interrogated, beaten for days, threatened and, finally, released. Once, soldiers came into his mother's house and destroyed everything inside. Jack was humiliated.

He was enraged with anger. He went wild. He began to hate Jews and Israelis. Looking back now he says, "I was only sixteen years old, but I was waiting for the moment I would die. I just knew I was going to die for a noble cause: so that my people might have freedom."

Though born into a Catholic family, Jack was a nonreligious, functional atheist. His grandfather had told him stories of fleeing the Turkish genocide in 1905, when 1.5 million Christians had been brutally dragged from their homes and killed. Jack had grown up in a dark cloud of racial injustice, hardship and violence.

Seven times Jack was imprisoned for crimes he never committed. One imprisonment was for three long months. He had been crammed into dirty cells with masses of people living in fear and treated without dignity. He had been beaten with belts and helmets. He was blindfolded, slapped with fists and open hands. He was inflicted with physical wounds that stirred hatred, frustration and rage within him.

"I saw my friends killed before my eyes," he elaborated. "I saw the pain my mother and sister felt, and I knew something had to change. Here I was, living on the Via Dolorosa, on the eighth station of the cross, where Jesus looked up and said, 'Women, don't cry for me. Daughters of Jerusalem, cry for your sons,' and yet I had not even been introduced to the One who was wounded for me. I was searching. I knew something had to change. Deep in my heart, I was desperate.

"One night I went to my friends, Yohanna and Haqib," he went on, "and that night they led me to Christ. The One who had walked the way of suffering for me came to my home to heal my own suffering soul. It was August 10, 1991, and God changed me inside. Instantly Jesus delivered me from drugs, and within a year, God delivered me from alcohol and smoking two packs of cigarettes a day. He changed my life because He changed my heart and my will."

Within three to four months Jack was in a prayer meeting where he was paired up with a Jewish, Messianic believer. The man said to him, "Jack, I want you to forgive me and my people for what they did to you. Are you willing to forgive me?" The question came like a slap to the face. Jack was quickly struck by how hot the hatred ran in his veins. He knew that though he wanted to forgive the man and the entire nation of Israel, he was unable to do so—or so he thought. "It suddenly hit me," Jack reflected, "that I was the one who needed to be forgiven. The hatred within my heart was still active within me; it was killing me. That day I repented, and I experienced deliverance from my human hatred. Jesus changed my will." Jack went on, "God used my Jewish brothers and sisters in my healing and my deliverance."

When Jack turned twenty, God filled him with the Holy Spirit, and the young man began to attend Bethlehem Bible College. President Bashar Awad became like a spiritual father to Jack. Brother Andrew, known publically as "God's smuggler," was also introduced to Jack and became a mentor in his life. Jack Sara was eventually asked to lead the only evangelical church in the Old City, the Jerusalem Alliance Church. Today he serves as president of Bethlehem Bible College and is one of the most influential Christian leaders in the Middle East. You can e-mail him at jack@bethbc.edu. He'd love to hear from you.

Jesus' surrender of His will in the garden of Gethsemane began the redemptive process that reshapes the will of people like Jack Sara. Your redemption also starts with your surrender. Jesus surrendered His will for you so that you might surrender your will to Him. His surrender invites your surrender.

But let's be honest—surrender is frightening. The thought of giving over control to someone else seems, at best, counterintuitive. We certainly need to know first that we can explicitly trust the one to whom we are asked to surrender. For this reason, we are told by the apostle John, "In this is love, not that we have loved God but that he loved us and sent his Son to be the propitiation for our sins."[13]

As you consider the wounds of Christ, don't miss the obvious: Each of His wounds are filled with love. His loving wounds are calling out to you. The wounds to His sweat glands are pleading for you to trust Him, and the healing of your will is at stake. As you think about it, you will soon find that you can trust Him, because He has already proven His love for you. Jesus did not come so much for religious people but for wounded people; and He wants you to know that He is ready, willing and able to heal your will today.

3

THE FACE OF JESUS
Recovering Our Identity

They spit in his face and struck him. And some slapped him.

Matthew 26: 67

The adult body has sixty thousand miles of blood vessels. It's hard to imagine, but we actually have so many veins, arteries and capillaries in our bodies that if they were somehow placed end to end, they would stretch around the earth at the equator two and a half times.

The blood itself is profoundly complex. Every second, four million red blood cells give up their lives to make our bodies function efficiently; and every second, exactly four million new blood cells leap from our bone marrow to continue the process. Every minute, our blood cells make a full circuit back to our hearts. Every red blood cell has a four-month lifespan and circles the body approximately two hundred thousand times. The internal purification of the body is highly sophisticated, and it all takes place because of the blood.

Without blood, poisons would pile up inside our bodies like garbage in the streets, since every organ in the body is constantly dumping toxic waste—carbon dioxide, urea and uric acid—into the blood stream and picking up fresh oxygen and fuel.

The heart is a ten-ounce muscle that contracts one hundred thousand times every day. It pumps two thousand gallons of blood around our circulatory system every day. In the course of a lifetime, it will beat two and a half billion times and pump the equivalent of sixty billion gallons of bloody fluid, seemingly without ever taking a break. Only three weeks after conception, a preborn baby has a faint heartbeat. At fourteen weeks following conception, the infant heart pumps the equivalent of seven gallons a day.

We do not normally view blood as a cleansing agent but as a staining agent. When we get blood on our hands or clothes, we use soap, water, disinfectant or detergent to wash it off as quickly as possible. Modern medicine, however, tells us what is counterintuitive—that rather than

being stained by blood, we are actually washed by blood.
This medical explanation of the cleansing process within
our physical bodies is a remarkably accurate picture of
a similar and parallel spiritual reality—we are actually
washed internally by the blood of Jesus.

We now move from the valley garden to the Jewish
temple, where Jesus received His second wound—the
wound to His face. The tranquility of the garden had
been disrupted by a hostile Jewish guard, and even
though it was the middle of the night, the place buzzed
and tempers ran hot. Jesus was no longer a free man. He
was treated like a rabid animal or a menace to society.
He no sooner surrendered His will than all hell seemed
to break loose! He was marched to the Temple where a
mock trial went from bad to worse; and soon, religious
power brokers were screaming at the top of their lungs,
hitting Jesus with their fists and spitting in His face.
Jesus was then taken to Pilate's palace where the
Romans continued the brutality by further marring
Jesus' face.

Our faces represent our identities and our dignity. To
lose face is to lose respect. To punch someone in the
face typically manifests anger. To slap someone in the
face shows disrespect. To hit someone in the face with
wooden branches is torturous. To spit on someone's
face shows abject contempt. Jesus experienced all this.

These blows to His face revealed anger, disrespect, torture and contempt. While Dr. Luke was the only Gospel writer to record the first wound to Jesus' sweat glands, all four Gospel writers included their own unique perspective on Christ's second wound. Like four videographers filming the same event, each with their own distinct camera angle, each of the four Gospel writers brought a distinct yet complementary perspective.

These face wounds of Jesus were brutally given in the Temple by the Jews and soon after in the palace of Pilate by the Romans. Matthew records, "They [the Jews] spit in his face and struck him. And some slapped him."[1] Matthew goes on to tell us, "They [the Romans] spit on him and took the reed and struck him on the head."[2] Mark records in his Gospel, "Some [Jews] began to spit on him and to cover his face and to strike him, saying to him, 'Prophesy!' And the guards received him with blows,"[3] and he continues, "They [Roman soldiers] were striking his head with a reed and spitting on him and kneeling down in homage to him."[4] Luke writes, "The men who were holding Jesus in custody were mocking him as they beat him."[5] And John records in his Gospel, "One of the officers [of the Jews] standing by struck Jesus with his hand."[6] Later John writes, "They [the Romans] came up to him, saying, 'Hail, King of the Jews!' and struck him with their hands."[7] When we put it all together, we can see in high-definition clarity that multiple times, with multiple means, both Jews and Romans spat on Jesus' face, slapped Him with their hands, hit Him with their fists and struck Him with sticks, leaving welts, gashes and mucus on His face.

CHRIST'S SURRENDER

As we have noted, every wound of Christ corresponds to a distinct act of surrender by Christ. With this second wound, Jesus actually surrendered face: His identity.

Jesus explicitly surrendered His face to be slapped with hands, hit with fists and struck with reeds because He voluntarily chose to surrender His identity. The prophet Isaiah wrote seven hundred years earlier in a prophetic declaration, "I gave . . . my cheeks to those who pull out the beard."[8] While none of the four Gospel writers include any record of Jesus' beard being plucked out, they certainly include many graphic examples of other blows to Christ's face. Jesus' surrender of identity in the final hours of His life was actually nothing new to Him—He had been living it out for thirty-three years. His father Joseph, at the news that Mary was pregnant, initially had no idea as to who this baby was and planned to dispose of Him quietly. After His birth, Jesus lived incognito with only a few people who knew

His true identity. Virtually no one, except in rare and fleeting moments, accurately recognized Jesus' true nature. Jesus certainly fulfilled the prophetic words of Isaiah: "He was despised and rejected by men . . . he was despised, and we esteemed him not."[9] As both Jews and Gentiles beat Jesus' face however, their torture went far beyond a failure to recognize Jesus' true identity. Christ was now not so much a victim of *mistaken* identity; He was more accurately a victim of *rejected* identity. To the extent that they knew who He was, they wanted Him gone.

Understand the irony of Jesus losing face. No one deserved more admiration, respect and appreciation than Jesus. No one knew His true identity better than Jesus Himself. That identity had been expressed by King David of the messianic Lord: "One thing I ask from the LORD, / this only do I seek: / that I may dwell in the house of the LORD / all the days of my life, / to gaze on the beauty of the LORD"[10] Yet despite His beauty, Christ voluntarily surrendered His identity and received the facial wounds of extreme disrespect, torture and contempt. The apostle Paul accurately described Christ's humiliation when he wrote, "Christ Jesus . . . though he was in the form of God, did not count equality with God a thing to be grasped, but emptied himself [made himself nothing]."[11]

OUR HEALING

As noted earlier, every wound of Christ corresponds to a wound in us. This wound to His face correlates with our wounds of disrespect, contempt and self-hatred.

Everyone struggles with identity issues. For many years, psychologists have been throwing around the statistic that 80 percent of women are consistently anxious and stressed-out about how they look. Recently, the cosmetic company Dove decided to sponsor a social experiment to test its accuracy. Their results were shown in a YouTube video that was watched by fifty million people in the first week or so, and an additional one hundred thirty million have seen it since. They hired FBI forensic artist Gil Zamora, who has over three thousand criminal sketches under his belt. He was asked to draw two sketches of a number of women, sight unseen. Gil was instructed to draw the first sketch by listening to the way the women described themselves, and the second according to the way a random stranger described them.

At the end of the experiment, every woman was handed the two drawings, and the results were shocking. In virtually every case, the picture drawn from the description of the total stranger was lifelike, realistic and accurate. The picture drawn from the woman's own description, on the other hand, was unkind, distorted, grossly overemphasizing a perceived flaw in her appearance. Zamora said, "I never imagined how different the two sketch portrayals would be. What has stayed with me are the emotional reactions the women had when they viewed the composite sketches side by side. I think many of these brave women realized that they had a distorted self-perception that had affected parts of their lives in significant ways."[12] You can view the YouTube video yourself. Just Google 'Real Beauty Sketches.'

As entertaining as this experiment was, most of us do not need a YouTube video to remind us of our unhealthy dose of low self-esteem. Restoring our self-worth and recovering our identities is part of why Christ came and why He died. More specifically, it is why Christ gave His face to those who spat, slapped, punched and hit Him with sticks. He took on Himself the wounds to our damaged dignity and lost identity.

We have each felt the wounds of mocking, shame, ridicule, personal failure and loss. Jesus lost face so that He could redeem ours. This was impressed on me one day as I visited a family in a children's hospital whose child had been diagnosed with meningitis—a diagnosis every parent dreads. I was not prepared for what I was about to encounter. As I entered the hospital, I passed a child without arms. As I got on the elevator, there sat a child with Down's syndrome. As I stepped off the elevator and looked into a room, there was a badly burned child. Suddenly my world was shaken. What dignity do these children have? I thought. Who will love and value them? Then I looked into the next room, and hanging on the wall was a large poster with words written in childlike crayon print that I will never forget.

I am somebody,
'cause God don't make no junk!

Those words seemed to stand out to me in neon lights. They reoriented my perspective. God created these children, like all people. Even if their bodies were badly damaged, they nevertheless carried the image of God within them. From the beginning, God said, "Let us make man in our image, after our likeness."[13] These special little ones, like all people, were valuable.

The stamp of God's image is on people like a VIN number on a car. The big difference, however, is that, unlike a car, we are completely unique from anyone else; and our souls, our spirits, are eternal. For this reason we can say to God with confidence the words of the ancient psalmist: "You formed my inward parts; / you knitted me together in my mother's womb. / I praise you, for I am fearfully and wonderfully made. / Wonderful are your works; / my soul knows it very well."[14]

A TWENTY-FIRST-CENTURY HEALING

When Nick was born on December 4, 1982, in Melbourne, Australia, his vital signs were perfect. His parents were so happy! There was just one noticeable abnormality—he had no arms and no legs. The three sonograms before his birth had failed to reveal any complications so there was no warning and no medical explanation.

Despite obvious challenges, Nick grew up with a keen intellect. He went to school and did well academically. One can only imagine, however, the amount of bullying he was forced to endure. The mocking became so severe that by the time he was ten, his self-esteem was shattered. He lived in the darkness of depression and loneliness and wondered why he was so different from his classmates. He cried out to God, "Why did you make me this way?"

He also questioned himself: "What's the point? Why am I here?" Adolescence is hard on every young person, but for Nick the issues were compounded. There was no hiding the fact that he was not like his peers. A few cruel kids dared to call him "freak" and "alien." Nick says of this time, "I hit a wall. My heart ached. I was depressed, overwhelmed with negative thoughts and didn't see any point in my life."[15]

At age fifteen Nick learned about Jesus and His wounds, and for the first time he experienced personally the love of God. He learned to trust God and even submitted his life to Him. His prayer changed from complaining to God about his too-obvious physical needs to asking God to help him with two deeper disabilities, ones we all share in common—the disabilities of sin and death.

When Nick was seventeen, a school janitor told him that despite his limitations, he would one day become a public speaker. As unlikely as this prediction seemed at the time, three months later Nick told the story of his own spiritual salvation in front of a group of ten classmates. It felt good. Soon Nick set his sights on becoming a public speaker.

At age twenty-one, he graduated as a CPA and financial planner. At age thirty, he married Kanae Miyahara. Nick and his wife now have two sons. Several years ago, he preached to three hundred fifty thousand people in a five-day period, and eighty thousand of them gave their lives to Christ. By 2013, Nick had preached to 450 million people in twenty-six different countries. He has now stood in front of eleven presidents and nine congressional groups. He's learned to swim, surf and skateboard. Christ lost face so that Nick and the rest of us can recover our true God-given identities. Nick now feels comfortable in his own skin because he has found his identity in Christ. Because he is in Christ, he knows that he is loved as Christ. To this day, he keeps a pair of shoes in his closet, because he's still asking God for a miracle. True story. Google "Nick Vujicic," and you will learn more about this inspiring, remarkable young man. What makes this man's true story possible are the wounds of Christ, specifically the wounds to Jesus' face.

What has it been for you? Bullying? Loneliness and depression? Insecurity or self-hatred? These are deep things, but as we've said, Jesus was not wounded so that He could maintain a superficial relationship with you. He wants to go deep with you. He wants to open you up to the dark, wounded places in your life. Best of all, He loves you. As the apostle John wrote, "We love because he [Jesus] first loved us."[1] This is the essence of Jesus' second wound. You too can learn firsthand that when you are in Christ, God loves you as Christ. If you trust Him, He can even teach you to love yourself for who you really are. In Christ, you are your best version of yourself.

4

THE BACK OF JESUS
Regaining Our Health

Pilate took Jesus and flogged him.

John 19:1

lagellation, or the practice of scourging, was a disgusting punishment. A short leather whip with bone or metal studs penetrated its victims' outer layer of skin and literally created ribbons of human flesh on their backs.

The Greek term for "scourged"[1] is *phragelloo*, which in Latin is translated *flagellum*, meaning "whip." While the Jews scourged their criminals with a penal thirty-nine lashes, the Romans were more excessive. When a criminal was assigned to execution, Roman scourging was a preliminary torture intended to weaken the victim *through shock and blood loss. Without scourging, a victim of crucifixion might remain on the cross for several days. With scourging, however, a victim died within a matter of hours.*

The Roman flagellum, or short whip, had a strong, thick handle with three thirty-inch strips of leather in which small iron balls or sharp, jagged pieces of sheep bone were tied at different intervals. The initial blows with the whip opened the victim's skin and underlying subcutaneous tissue, ripping into the paraspinal muscles on the back as well as the serratus anterior muscle and the trapezius and latissimus dorsi. Subsequent blows tattered the underlying pectoralis major and pectoralis minor muscles as the whip strands wrapped around the back and reached the chest. Once these layers were ravaged, repetitive blows could cut through the three layers of intercostal muscles, causing the superficial and cutaneous vessels of the trunk to be lacerated. The victim's blood loss was substantial, and the person's lacerated, bloody skin literally looked like shredded meat.

Walking down the Via Dolorosa, the path of pain, from Pilate's palace where Jesus' death sentence was given, we arrive at the scene of Christ's third wound—the wound to His back. We climb down the flight of stairs once again to the stone chamber forty-five feet underground, and we gather around the Roman whipping stone, likely the historic location where Jesus was scourged. Roman flogging was one of the most hideous forms of brutality and torture ever invented. The violent act pierced a person's outer tissue of skin, sinking into the muscle tissue and ripping open the flesh. Some people mistakenly think that Christ only received thirty-nine lashes. Not true. While it was Jewish custom to administer no more than thirty-nine lashes, the scourging of Christ was done by the far less civilized Romans. The Romans' objective was not simply to punish their victims but to prepare them for quicker death. They intentionally drained as much blood and life out of a victim as possible prior to crucifixion so that the person would die more quickly.

It is also incorrectly believed that flagellation was done only across Jesus' upper back or shoulders. No such luck! Roman flagellation was done across a person's entire back side (even wrapped around to the chest)—the lower neck, upper back, back of the arms, lower back, buttocks, thighs, calves and all the way down to the ankles.

CHRIST'S SURRENDER

These wounds to Christ's back, like the others, were an intentional act of submission on His part. They represent His surrender of His physical health. Seven hundred years before the death of Christ, Isaiah prophesied, "I gave my back to those who strike."[2] This was written long before the flagellum was even invented. Notice the voluntary choice Christ made—"I gave my back to those who strike." When Christ voluntarily submitted His back to scourging, it was brutal. Grotesque. Hideous. It is impossible to overstate the torment Jesus endured at the Roman whipping stone. Most of us can't help but wince when we consider the strips of leather with their jagged teeth wrapping around Jesus' body and cutting into His flesh.

Jesus' act of determination is modeled by the Navy SEALs. Two of the most decorated Navy SEALs, Jocko Willink and Leif Babin, wrote a book, *Extreme Ownership*, in which they recorded the twelve principles by which the SEALs operate. Every principle reinforces the central theme that separates Navy SEALs from all other enlisted people: extreme ownership. Extreme ownership means that one doesn't pass the buck, doesn't point fingers nor blame anyone else. Instead, one takes responsibility. Every member of the Navy SEAL group assumes 100 percent responsibility not only for themselves but also for everyone else on their team. Just imagine serving on a team that actually practiced this principle! No one in history ever took 100 percent responsibility for himself and his teammates the way Jesus did.

Roman flagellum

OUR HEALING

As we have seen, every wound in Christ corresponds to a wound in us. As we investigate the severity of Jesus' third wound, the logical question that demands an answer is, why? Why did Christ give His back to those who struck Him? What is the point of the gruesome mutilation to His back?

The prophet Isaiah answered this question with pinpoint accuracy: "Surely he took up our pain / and bore our suffering,"[3] and, "With his wounds [stripes/flagellation] we are healed."[4] These verses make it clear that the scourging of Christ's back was not only to purchase forgiveness for our sins but also to gain healing for our physical wounds, sicknesses and diseases.

Some have tried to debate this point, arguing that Isaiah 53 refers to spiritual rather than physical healing. Not so fast. It is normally best to allow the Bible to interpret itself. In his Gospel, Matthew makes it very clear that the Isaiah prophecy is in fact referring to physical healing: "That evening they brought to him many . . . and [he] healed all who were sick. This was to fulfill what was spoken by the prophet Isaiah: 'He took our illnesses and bore our diseases.'"[5] This means that the innumerable wounds on Jesus' back correspond to the innumerable wounds, illnesses and diseases in us. Christ surrendered His perfect physical health in order to take extreme ownership for our physical diseases. He specifically took our heart, liver, lung, kidney and mental diseases, as well as any other kind of physical disease. Migraines, autism, addictions, diabetes, scoliosis, lupus, cancers, bipolar disorder—you name it, He took it. He exerted extreme ownership.

Divine healing is a benefit of Christ's atonement that is as much for us today as it was during Christ's ministry two thousand years ago. These flagellation wounds were embedded deep in Jesus' physical body, and they include healing to the diseases and wounds in our physical bodies. As the Bible says, "The body is . . . for the

Lord, and the Lord for the body."[6] There is no need to make divine healing too complicated.

The reason there is so much confusion over divine healing is that there are many streams of false teaching on this subject. We need to clarify that divine healing is not mental or metaphysical healing like that done by a Jedi Master playing mind games.

We can repeat the mantra "I am not sick, I am not sick, I am not sick" all we want, but empty repetition will not bring about divine healing. Divine healing is not willpower either, as if we could demand our own healing. Neither does divine healing come by saying enough prayers, conjuring up enough faith, or getting enough signatures on a petition to bring God to some magical tipping point.

No, divine healing is not the work of our minds, our wills or even our faith. Divine healing is the work of God in Christ. Jesus is the one who took up our sorrows and carried our diseases; and by His scourging alone, we may be healed. True divine healing comes as a result of the wounds of Christ, the blood of Christ, the life of Christ and the resurrection of Christ. The apostle Paul emphasized Jesus' healing when he wrote, "If the Spirit of him who raised Jesus from the dead dwells in you, he who raised Christ Jesus from the dead will also give life to your mortal bodies through his Spirit who dwells in you."[7]

In addition to giving physical healing to us before we die, the wounds of Christ will eventually bring life back to dead bodies as well. When Christ returns, He will reunite every human spirit with its physical, resurrected body. This wild moment of resurrection will be one of the ultimate victory realities in life and it too was purchased by the wounds of Christ.

A TWENTY-FIRST-CENTURY HEALING

Susana had worn coke-bottle-bottom glasses since she was eight years old. Because of her astigmatism, her bad eyesight was degenerative, and she had been visually challenged her entire adult life. As a seamstress and an employee at a fabric store, she was dependent on reading glasses. These were her only corrective option, as she lived on a tight budget, and it was hard for her to function without them. One day the unthinkable happened—Susana broke her only pair of reading glasses! "Oh, no!" she gasped. "What am I to do?" She panicked. Without money to purchase another pair, she was in a crisis. What made matters worse is that not wearing her glasses gave her extreme headaches.

While standing in the kitchen, Susana told her daughter, "Mommy's glasses broke this week. We need God to solve this problem so I can continue to work."

Her daughter, Tammy, asked if God could make her eyes all better, but Susana's unbelief sent her mind into a tailspin: How do I answer this without crushing her faith? What if God doesn't answer her little prayer? I just can't imagine God healing my eyes, but I don't want my daughter's faith to be damaged. What will I tell my daughter when I'm not healed? That is all she could think, but out loud Susana said to her daughter, "God can provide the money for new glasses, and He can heal my eyes through medicine and doctors."

Tammy responded, "But Mom, can't God make your eyes better all by Himself?"

"Well, yes, He can," Susana conceded.

Before she could finish the sentence, little Tammy jumped in with a prayer. It was short and sweet and remarkably to the point: "Lord, make Mom's eyes better, in Jesus' name. Amen!" Tammy turned and bounded out of the kitchen before Susana was able to prepare her daughter for what she thought was inevitable disappointment. The next day at the fabric store, a customer needed help reading the extra-fine print on the back of a sewing pattern. Susana looked at the back of the pattern—and read it without any difficulty. She was instantly shaken. "I can see. I can read—perfectly!"

She was humbled. Overwhelmed. "I stopped in my tracks. I was instantly convicted over my unbelief. Here my daughter had exhibited perfect faith, and I hadn't believed for a moment that I would ever be healed. I had been more concerned about how I would walk my daughter through her disappointment," she explained. "Of course, I knew that God could do anything, but I never expected Him to heal me. Not now. Not like this. And that's when I learned what it's like to go to God in prayer with faith like a child."

While I have witnessed literally thousands of divine healings, I selected this story, not only because it is medically verifiable, but also because it shows the loving, compassionate hand of God at work in the lives of a precious family. Does Jesus automatically heal everyone? Certainly not. When we pray for healing in our church, we explain it this way: "We don't promise you healing, but we promise you Jesus. He loves you, and He is a healer. Let's ask Him to come and manifest His love to you. Let's see what He might do." Susana's healing happened ten years ago, and I spoke with Susana yesterday—her eyesight is still perfect. Her name is Susana Jaruczyk, she lives in Atlanta, Georgia, and to this day, she can still read the fine print!

What is it for you? Migraines, allergies or scoliosis? Whatever physical illness you have, Jesus can heal today. I can't promise you healing, but I promise you Jesus, and He is a healer.

With all He suffered for you in order to take your diseases, you do not want His healing to remain unused. If you walked into a pharmacy and knew there was a medication there that would cure you, you certainly wouldn't leave the medicine sitting on the shelf. You would take it to the clerk and purchase it. It is the same with divine healing! You can, by the grace of God, appropriate the cure. The only difference is that when you step to the counter to check out, you will find that Jesus is your physician and that, in His great love for you, He has already paid in full for your medication. You can trust Him. He loves you, and He will do for you what is best.

5

THE HEAD OF JESUS
Reclaiming Our Dignity

*They stripped him and put a scarlet robe on him, and
twisting together a crown of thorns, they put it on his head.*

Matthew 27: 28–29

The cardiovascular system in the head is one of the most sophisticated systems in the body. While oxygenated blood is carried to the brain by four major arteries, deoxygenated blood is taken from the head by three major veins. A sophisticated system branches off to form an external labyrinth of blood vessels to the superficial structures of the head.

Twelve major pairs of nerves called cranial nerves—which control smell, sight, contraction of eye muscles, sensory and motor nerves of the face and head, facial *expressions, hearing and equilibrium from the inner ear, taste, the use of the tongue and larynx, and the movements of the neck and throat—are all connected to the brain. When the thorns punctured the skin around the circumference of Jesus' head, masses of nerve endings and a whole labyrinth of blood vessels were violated.*

Near the Roman whipping stone, soldiers deviously twisted together a mocking crown of thorns.[1] Following Christ's brutal flagellation, the soldiers took Jesus to the governor's headquarters and paraded Him in front of a battalion of about five hundred men. They stripped Him of His outer clothing, draped a robe over His mangled shoulders, and put an unspeakably sharp crown of thorns on His head.[2] These thorns gave Jesus His fourth wound.

Those who are familiar with Jesus' story may take for granted the crown of thorns, thinking that everyone who was crucified was crowned this way. Not so. In fact, Jesus may have been the only one to wear such a crown. While the Romans crucified thousands, and flogged tens of thousands, they may well have placed a crown of thorns on the head of only one person— Jesus. He was, after all, the only one mockingly accused of being King of the Jews.

Botanists familiar with foliage in the Middle East have suggested that the thorns most likely came from the lote tree, scientifically known as the *ziziphus spina-christi*. The tree has thorns that average one inch in length, and they are as strong as steel.[3] This crown, or helmet, probably covered Jesus' entire scalp. Gospel accounts indicate that Jesus continued to receive head blows even after He was scourged, and these blows would have driven the thorns deeply into His heavily bleeding forehead, penetrating both the *frontalis* and *occipitalis* muscles. With the numerous arterial and venous tributaries encircling the surface of the scalp, Jesus' bleeding would have been profuse. With the density of surface nerves, His pain would have been indescribable.

A crown is normally a distinguishing symbol of honor, glory and power. It reflects the value given to the one wearing it. It is easy to recall impressive crowns throughout history. The Czech Republic owns the Bohemian crown, a 22-karat gold crown with an assortment of almost one hundred jewels. Denmark has a solid-gold crown weighing an impressive 6 pounds, 6 ounces. Bulgaria has an elaborate set of crowns valued at $17 million. Austria keeps its crown jewels in the Imperial Treasury in Vienna, and this crown holds a single 36-carat diamond worth in excess of $16 million. The priciest crown of all is owned by Queen Elizabeth of England—boasting five rubies, eleven emeralds, seventeen sapphires, three hundred pearls and an astounding three thousand diamonds. The largest and heaviest crown was worn by King Tupu IV, ruler of Tonga, the smallest country in the world, in the South Pacific islands. His crown weighed an overwhelming 460 pounds, 13 ounces. Several servants were required to stand on either side of the Tonga king's head to keep the crown from snapping his neck.

These opulent crowns stand in stark contrast to Christ's crown of thorns. Though Jesus could easily and rightfully have worn a crown that would have made all others look like rhinestones and costume jewelry, this was not His mission. He came not simply to show His glory but to surrender it so that we could regain our lost glory.

CHRIST'S SURRENDER

When Christ was crowned with thorns, He surrendered His own glory, honor and dignity. Nothing more graphically portrays human misery than thorns and thistles, and nowhere on Christ's body would the thorns have created a harsher contrast with Christ's beauty than on His lovely head.

When the mocking crowd crowned Jesus with thorns, it was a disgusting, horrifying sight. Just think of it— Jesus is, after all, King of heaven, King of the Jews, King of the nations, King of creation and King of Glory. He is actually the Son of God, the creator of all things, who came to live on earth, and yet He was ruthlessly mocked and brutalized by the very people He came to redeem. To better understand this particular step of surrender, we need to go back into history thousands of years.

Soon after the fall of humanity, God announced to Adam, "Cursed is the ground because of you; / in pain you shall eat of it all the days of your life; / thorns and thistles it shall bring forth for you; / and you shall eat the plants of the field."[4] The source of thorns and thistles was this curse on the earth, which came from an act of disobedience. The irreverent, disrespectful Roman soldiers had probably never read the book of Genesis and never considered the connection between the thorns and the sin of humanity. They obviously had no intention of making a prophetic symbol to place on Jesus' head. Nevertheless, the thorns placed on Christ's head in preparation for His execution could not have made a more accurate image of earth's curse. Jesus' crown of thorns created the vivid image that Christ took the full weight of the curses of fallen humanity on Himself. The thorns on Jesus' head created a ring of puncture wounds in Jesus' scalp.

As a side note, the Shroud of Turin is worth studying in this regard. Much evidence points to the strong possibility that this single piece of linen, preserved by the church through the ages, may well have been the actual seamless cloth that was wrapped around the mutilated, dead body of Christ and remained in the tomb following Jesus' resurrection.[5] Perhaps one of the most convincing arguments for this is that the shroud shows the marks of distinct puncture wounds around the forehead of the facial silhouette on the cloth. While these markings do not emphatically prove that the Shroud of Turin is the very linen that was wrapped around Jesus' body, they do indicate that it very well could have been. Given the fact that we have no known record of a crown of thorns ever being used on another victim of crucifixion, it certainly raises the likelihood.

When Jesus wore the mocking purple robe and the disgraceful crown of thorns, Pilate issued a prophetic declaration that has reverberated throughout the ages—"Behold the man!"[6] Whatever he meant by this, the Roman leader could not have been more accurate. Jesus was the man—the representative man who embodied the wounds of all humanity and took on His head the disgrace and shame of us all.

OUR HEALING

This fourth wound of Jesus, the wound to His head, corresponds to our own damaged self-worth. When we are mocked, devalued and underappreciated, the pain we feel is, at times, intolerable. Few things in life puncture our dignity as deeply as insults. We have all felt them. When these wounds accumulate and fester with infection, they can bring any of us to self-hatred. We have all been wounded, and we all need healing.

English poet John Milton wrote his epic twelve-volume poem *Paradise Lost* in 1674. It contains a whopping ten thousand lines of poetic verse; and following the biblical story of the tragedy of Adam and Eve and their expulsion from the garden, it dramatically captures the plight of humanity and human suffering. Milton accurately describes Adam and Eve's difficulty: While they never lost God's love, they certainly forfeited God's presence. Reclaiming the relationship with God's presence is the essence of why Jesus came.

Christ surrendered His honor in order to redeem our honor. The psalmist grabbed hold of healing for his self-esteem when he cried, "You, O LORD, are a shield about me, / my glory, and the lifter of my head."[7] Christ's head bowed in shame under the crown of thorns so that He might restore our honor and so that each of us can call Him "the lifter of my head." The thorns represent not only the curse on each of us personally but also on the earth and the entire created universe. When Christ wore the crown of thorns, it represented the fact that Christ's atonement will, in the future, redeem both individual people and all creation. One day Christ will create a thoroughly new heaven and new earth, and the first heaven and the first earth will pass away;[8] but today, the entire created universe is groaning and creaking like an old ship in a storm. The apostle Paul wrote, "Not only the creation, but we ourselves, who have the firstfruits of the Spirit, groan inwardly as we wait eagerly for the adoption as sons, the redemption of our bodies."[9] The groaning of creation is seen everywhere in society today—in ISIS and militant jihadist Islam, in nuclear threats from Iran and North Korea, in the medical epidemics of AIDS, SARS, Ebola and Zika, and so much more. But Christ was wounded and gained healing for us as individuals and for all creation, and He will one day create for Himself a new heaven and a new earth.

The apostle Paul effectively described this full scope of Christ's redemption.

He is the image of the invisible God, the firstborn of all creation. For by him all things were created, in heaven and on earth, visible and invisible, whether thrones or dominions or rulers or authorities—all things were created through him and for him. And he is before all things, and in him all things hold together. And he is the head of the body, the church. He is the beginning, the firstborn from the dead, that in everything he might be preeminent. For in him all the fullness of God was pleased to dwell, and through him to reconcile to himself all things, whether on earth or in heaven, making peace by the blood of his cross.[10]

A TWENTY-FIRST-CENTURY HEALING

Christy is a beautiful woman; but when we first met her, she was anything but a pretty sight. She lay on the floor crying uncontrollably, and none of us standing near her in the auditorium knew why. "We need your help," her husband, Chip, begged. "Would you come with me? Let's bring her into the side room and see what we can do." We soon learned that Christy was suffering from depression—deep depression.

Looking at her life, it didn't make sense that she would be suffering so deeply. Christy had grown up in a small town with a loving family. She had married her best friend and was on an incredible journey with three precious children, a beautiful home and even a cute dog. She had everything a girl could dream of, but deep inside she was in the middle of an emotional and spiritual war. As a little girl, she was often overcome with fear and loneliness. A voice in her head told her she would never be good enough, strong enough or talented enough. She battled fear. At age fourteen, she met Jesus and surrendered her life to Him. Little insecurities, however, kept creeping back into her life. She felt rejection and despair. When she and Chip started having babies, she experienced tremendous bouts of postpartum depression. Fear, guilt and insecurities flooded her mind. You can't handle this. You should be happy. Your family deserves better. Torturing thoughts flooded her mind and ruthlessly accused her. Christy was eventually diagnosed with clinical depression and spent the next ten years medicating her symptoms. Life was a bit more tolerable, but she was emotionally numb and terrified of the medication's side effects. After taking it for some time, the medicine was no longer enough. Christy's anxiety disorder left her with such insecurity and feelings of inferiority that she did not even feel loved by God. She felt sad, defeated, isolated and hopeless.

One day in 2012, she attended the first module of the College of Prayer in Brandon, Mississippi. During a public service with a couple hundred other people, Christy took a sincere look at her heart and life; and by the love of God and the grace of Jesus, she took authority over the evil forces trying to destroy her and broke the curse she'd been living under her whole life. This began a redemptive process of healing her self-worth that continues to this day. Describing the experience,

Christy said, "For the first time ever, I felt hope that through the redemptive healing work of Jesus, I could overcome. I cast off religious excellence and the costume of perfection. Since then, I have been on a new path in His presence where there is fullness of joy, peace and freedom."

Christy is a work in process. Like many of us, her healing is coming one step at a time; and, thankfully, she continues to put one foot in front of the other in the right direction. But it's all because of Jesus' wounds, particularly the wound to His head. Jesus abandoned His own dignity in order to reclaim Christy's dignity. You can watch Christy Henderson tell her own story by visiting http://pinelake.org/stories/a-war-in-my-soul/.

Christy told me yesterday, "I wish I could say I never have bad days, but that's not true. I am, however, constantly relying on God's Spirit to strengthen, protect and deliver me. And He has been faithful." She went on, "I am now an overcomer. I am free. I know I am loved, and I am liberated. Even my tongue has been set free. I can speak into so many women's lives. God said to me, 'Christy, you're not a nobody. You're my chosen one. You are significant.'"

Wounds tend to define us. The wounded wound, and the healed heal. The hated hate, and the loved love. The cursed curse, and the blessed bless. Those who have themselves been hurt will often hurt others or even hurt themselves. God wants you to know by experience that He sent Jesus to take all your wounds and curses. He wants to now give you His blessings. Jesus specifically took the wounds to your self-worth so that you might regain your true dignity in Christ. "God shows his love for us in that while we were still sinners, Christ died for us," wrote the apostle Paul.[11] Jesus was wounded for you when He wore your crown so that He can now be the lifter of your head. Christy learned this by experience, and you can too.

6

THE HANDS OF JESUS
Reestablishing Our Productivity

They have pierced my hands and feet.

Psalm 22:16

One-third of the touch receptor nerves of the entire body are in the hand. Oxygenated blood flows through two subclavian arteries that travel through the wrist. The dorsal venous network of veins spreads out across the back of the hand and returns blood to the heart to be reoxygenated.

Three sets of nerves serve the hand, including the ulnar nerve that travels through the elbow, or the "funny bone," and serves the ring finger and pinky; the radial nerve that runs through the triceps and branches across the back of the hand beginning at the wrist; and the median nerve *that begins at the upper arm and serves the thumb, index and middle fingers. All the nerves and blood vessels travel through the wrist, which is where Jesus received His fifth wound.*

Historical research into Roman accounts has established that during the barbaric practice of crucifixion the nails were driven not into a victim's palms, as they would have ripped out between the fingers when made to support the weight of the human body, but rather between the wrist bones—the radius and ulna.

As we leave the Old City through a gate in the wall, we arrive at the place called "the hill of the skull," or Golgotha. This is the scene of the actual crucifixion, and we will be here through each of Jesus' final wounds. Jesus was escorted outside the city walls to be executed because religious law stipulated that the holy city of Jerusalem could not be defiled by crucifixion. With four brutal wounds already inflicted, it is here that Jesus received His final three wounds, and the wounding here started with His hands.

One Roman soldier grabbed Jesus' forearms and stretched them out along the top of the cross, almost as if pinning an insect to a display case or preparing an animal for dissection in biology class. It was ugly. Abusive. Unjust. Unthinkable. The grotesque Roman practice of death by crucifixion continued as another soldier grabbed a well-worn hammer and a large nail similar to a half-inch-thick rebar and drove it through Jesus' wrists, deep into the wooden plank that formed the crossbeam. Christ's other wrist was then driven through in the same way.

CHRIST'S SURRENDER

Roman nail

This fifth wound of Christ corresponds to Jesus' surrender of His work. Jesus said to His Father God in prayer, "I glorified you on earth, having accomplished the work that you gave me to do."[1] On another occasion He said, "My food is to do the will of him who sent me and to accomplish his work."[2] He would go on to say from the cross, "It is finished."[3] Despite the abusive degradation of the moment when the soldiers barbarically drove the nails into Jesus' hands, don't miss the critical issue: Christ voluntarily submitted to these nails. As He had already said, "I lay down my life. . . . No one takes it from me."[4]

We must understand that these hands that were punctured were the kind, compassionate, healing hands of Jesus. These hands had touched and healed a man with a speech impediment. On another day, they had dared to touch an untouchable leper and heal him. On another occasion, these hands touched Peter's feverish mother-in-law and immediately healed her. They touched a dead daughter's hand and raised the girl to her feet. When Jesus walked on the surface of the Sea of Galilee, these hands grabbed the hand of His sinking friend, Peter, and raised him up to safety. On a different day, when asked for help by a blind man, Jesus spit on the ground, made mud, and these healing hands placed the mud on the man's eyes and healed him. Jesus spread these hands out when He said to the crowds, "Come to me, all who labor and are heavy laden, and I will give you rest."[5] With His hands, Jesus had taken bread and broken it and said, "This is my body."[6] These hands had healed the sick, comforted the grieving, lifted the fallen, touched the untouchable and raised the dead. But now these hands were pierced with Roman nails, and Jesus' work—His productivity—was surrendered.

OUR HEALING

This fifth wound of Christ corresponds to the wound of our own hands—the wound of ineffectiveness or unproductivity.

We all have the will to be productive, to achieve and make our mark. For most of us, our work ethic is inseparably linked to our self-esteem and self-worth. When our hands are full of productivity, our hearts are normally full of joy. There is just one problem: The link between our hands and our hearts has been damaged by our own failure, and the work of our hands has become ineffective and unproductive. Therefore, all too often, our hearts are unfulfilled. Disappointment, discouragement and depression are the result.

In the beginning, God said to the first people in the garden of Eden, "Have dominion over the fish of the sea and over the birds of the heavens and over every living thing that moves on the earth."[7] He also set a loving boundary to protect men and women, saying, "You may surely eat of every tree in the garden, but of the tree of the knowledge of good and evil you shall not eat, for in the day that you eat of it you shall surely die."[8] It didn't take long, however, for their hands to break the rules. They grabbed, in their hands, the forbidden fruit, and this action proved to be deadly—Adam and Eve forfeited their productivity and thus their fulfillment. They turned the fertile garden into a broken dream. From this historic moment, humanity has lived with the lingering reality that we should be doing better.

This is precisely why Christ stretched out His hands on the cross and received the nails in His wrists, surrendering His productivity. He linked Himself with this wound in our twisted humanity. He intentionally took hold of this curse of our unproductivity and unfulfillment in order to redeem the work of our hands.

Let's admit it—most of us work hard. We take seriously the work of our hands and our responsibilities. This makes it difficult for us to open our hands and relinquish control. As a young father, I learned a remarkable lesson about the importance of what is in our hands. Our eighteen-month-old son came running up to us in the kitchen with a huge smile on his face as he lifted his hand toward us to show us the trophy in his fist. We were horrified to see what he was holding—a large carving knife with a supersharp edge. His little fingers tightly gripped the shiny blade. My wife screamed. As I reached for the knife, his little fingers tightened even more around the blade. We both panicked. What instantly became a game to him was no laughing matter to his mother and me. As his loving father, I had to reason with him and convince him that someday he could hold a knife like that, but not today. He wasn't ready. He needed to release his grip on the blade and give it to me. I desperately used every negotiating skill known to man! Before long, he relinquished the blade and the crisis was averted. I'm not sure he learned a lesson, but I sure did—don't leave the knife drawer open for a little toddler to test his reach.

Similarly, we all from time to time hold potentially dangerous things in the vise grip of our clenched fists —things that may be essentially good but, at the wrong time, can also destroy us if we are not equipped to handle them. We are talking about things like careers, our life purpose and our destiny. Our loving Father reasons with us and consistently attempts to convince us that He alone can coach us in these big life-issue moments and redeem the work of our hands.

A TWENTY-FIRST-CENTURY HEALING

Al was in crisis. As a professional cartoonist, he had established himself as a successful artist for Marvel Comics, yet his marriage and family were on the brink of disaster. What do I do? Where do I turn? he thought. He found himself feeling hopeless and groping for answers in what seemed like an empty universe.

He had drawn SpiderMan, the Hulk, Sergeant Fury, and a host of other superhero cartoon characters; but in his own personal life, he felt nothing like a superhero. While Al certainly was not a religious man, in desperation he made a phone call to line up an appointment with someone who had been referred to him as a "good guy and Christian counselor."

That day proved revolutionary. Al revealed his own life to the counselor like an open book, and the counselor offered rock-solid perspective: "Al, you've told me your story, now I need to tell you Jesus' story." In the next forty-five minutes, a transition took place that forever changed not only Al's life, but also the lives of his family members, community members and hundreds of thousands of people around the world.

"I want to introduce you, Al, to Jesus," the counselor began. "While I'm certain you've heard of Him, I'm equally certain you don't know Him. You see, Al, you have been in control of your life; and by your own admission, you've made a mess of things." Al nodded in agreement. "When Jesus voluntarily went to the cross, He did it to pay the debt for your sins; and in the process, His hands were pierced, and He relinquished control over His own work. His hands were wounded because your hands were wounded. Jesus now wants to be your wounded healer. Jesus abandoned the work of His hands when He chose the cross, but He did it in order to redeem and reestablish the work of your hands. This is what it means for Jesus to truly be your Redeemer. He chose the cross, where He both surrendered His productivity and received your unproductivity."

It made sense to Al.

Following a pensive pause, the counselor added, "The good news of Jesus is that His wounds are now healed. In fact, they are healed, and they are healing. Al, Jesus' hands can heal you too. You are an artist, but so is God—in fact, He's the master artist and you are like a canvas on His easel. He wants to make your life a masterpiece. There is just one issue—you need to quit fighting and running. You need to submit to Him and allow Him to finish the portrait He is sketching of your life."

That's all it took. Al knelt right there in the counselor's office and prayed to God a prayer of surrender, relinquishment and confession. He exchanged the broken pieces of his life for the healing presence of Christ. A new life was born that day.

Within a week, a phone call came from John Goldwater of Archie Comics. For the first time in his illustrious career, a major cartoon company recruited Al. He started work immediately. The Archie characters' personalities fit Al's playful sense of humor perfectly. In no time, Al became one of the most productive and admired artists. He was one of Archie Comics' only artists who both wrote and illustrated the stories.

Al's creativity and productivity soon increased. He got up early every morning, prayed to the Lord first thing for creativity and inspiration, wrote a story before breakfast, and had it laid out and sketched in pencil before noon. Increasingly Al included Bible verses and Christian principles in his stories. Betty became a Christian in Al's stories, as did Archie. Big Ethel, who frequently struggled with low self-esteem, found peace of mind in the fact that she was created in the image of God. Because his work was fun, wholesome and creative, his boss never complained. But when in a Christmas comic book, Betty, Veronica, Archie, Reggie, Moose and Jughead all knelt in prayer around a public manger scene, once again the phone rang. "Al," Mr. Goldwater said after reading the story, "we are publishing comic books, not the Bible! Your artwork is superior, and we don't want to lose you as an artist, but you need to tone it down." Point taken.

Within a month, Fleming H. Revell Company, a Christian publishing house, approached Al and pursued a partnership with him. Mr. Goldwater was glad to negotiate the publishing agreement. Over the next twenty years, Al wrote, drew and inked more than sixty-five Christian comic books, all published by Archie Comics under the Spire Christian Comic book label—including *Archie's One Way*, *David Wilkerson's The Cross and the Switchblade*, *Hello, I'm Johnny Cash*, and a host of others. Some sold several million copies, making Al's comics some of the highest-selling comic books in history. In 1980, Al received the distinguished Ink Pot Award of Achievement, the highest award given in the comic-book industry.

I know all this because Al Hartley was my dad. I witnessed firsthand the dramatic and miraculous change the wounds of Christ made in his life. My dad was asked to speak at my high school on the topic of "Cartoons, Creativity and Christ" during my senior year in Morristown, New Jersey. My friends loved it. I will never forget the message he gave my classmates that day: how Jesus redeemed the work of his hands.

Jesus loves you, and He is ready and able to redeem you from past failures and reestablish your productivity. Until the wounds of your heart and hands are healed, you will never know true fulfillment. No matter how excruciating the pain you have felt over your failures in the past, God knows how you feel today. The word "excruciating" refers to something that causes great agony and torment. It comes from the Latin root *ex-cruciate*, or "out of the cross." Jesus suffered excruciating pain in His wrists in order to heal both your hand wounds of unproductivity and your heart wounds of unfulfillment. You can trust Him.

7

THE FEET OF JESUS
Restoring Our Authority

He shall bruise your head, and you shall bruise his heel.

Genesis 3: 15

A blood transfusion is a safe, routine medical procedure that can be lifesaving. In times of critical surgery, injury, bleeding or disease, or when the body is incapable of producing enough of its own blood because of illness, a blood transfusion is vital to help a person avoid anemia, or lack of sufficient blood. The transfusion is normally administered through an intravenous line to a blood vessel.

A willing person donates blood for the benefit of others. At times, a transfusion is done to supplement certain components in a person's blood with these donated blood products, including red cells, white cells, plasma and platelets. While researchers are working diligently to create artificial blood, so far, no adequate replacement has been developed.

Five million blood transfusions are administered each year; most go well, with very few complications, as long as the blood type is matched properly. In simple terms, every person has one of only a few possible blood types: A, B, AB or O. If a person has type A blood, it is either A positive or A negative. It is essential during a transfusion that a donor's blood type matches that of the person receiving the blood. Type O blood is called the universal donor and is safe for virtually everyone. In emergencies, when there is no time to test a person's blood type, type O blood is used.

The common, safe and lifesaving medical procedure of a blood transfusion has a dramatic parallel to a spiritual reality: We all are in need of an internal moral and spiritual blood transfusion; and Jesus is, for all humankind, the universal donor.

On "the hill of the skull," outside the Old City gates where Jesus' crucifixion had begun, the Roman soldiers who had driven the metal rebar through Jesus' wrists next stretched out His left foot and pressed it backward against His right foot, with both feet extended, toes down. They brutally drove a single large nail through the arch of the front foot and out through the heel, through the arch in the right foot and out through the heel, and into the wooden plank. This nail through the meat of Jesus' heel actually provided Jesus the ability to support the weight of His body while hanging from the wooden beam. This sixth wound of Jesus completed the torturous process of His crucifixion.

CHRIST'S SURRENDER

This wound of Christ to His feet corresponds to the intentional surrender of His authority, territory and dominion. What makes this sixth wound so extraordinary is that these are the same feet that literally walked on water and figuratively exercised authority over the devil. There is a reason for such an unlikely wound.

Thousands of years earlier, when God spoke a rebuke to the serpent in the garden, He said, "I will put enmity between you and the woman, / and between your offspring and her offspring; / he shall bruise your head, / and you shall bruise his heel."[1] This is the first promise in the Bible that tells us that a messiah or savior would come to rescue humanity from the curse. In this single sentence, we are given a remarkably clear prophecy about a child—a young man, to be more precise— who would crush the serpent's head, and somehow the serpent would simultaneously bruise the young man's heel. This sentence also vividly describes the sixth wound. The young man, Jesus, would be wounded in His heel when the old Roman nail was driven clear through it; and at the same moment, Satan's power and authority would be broken. The bruising of the Messiah's heel was fulfilled on the cross, and simultaneously the same wound gave a mortal blow to Satan's head. A thousand years before the birth of Jesus, King David wrote the prophetic words, "Dogs encompass me; / a company of evildoers encircles me; / they have pierced my hands and feet."[2] The one who had all rightful authority, dominion and territory, the one of whom it was said, "The earth is the LORD's, and everything in it,"[3] is the one who had now surrendered all His rightful territory.

OUR HEALING

While Jesus' fifth wound to His hands represented the curse on our productivity, this sixth wound to His feet links to our abdication of our God-given authority. God made humankind to have dominion over the earth, and the picture in Scripture of authority is represented by having things under our feet: "What is man, that you are mindful of him, / or the son of man, that you care for him? / You made him for a little while lower than the angels; / you have crowned him with glory and honor, / putting everything in subjection under his feet."[4]

Humankind has dropped the ball. We have fumbled the proper use of our leadership, the stewardship of our resources, and our moral and spiritual authority.

Perhaps nothing better illustrates the abdication of moral authority than the infamous decline of the Roman Empire. Despite the fact that Rome had raised the global standards of art, drama, literature, architecture, wealth, roads, transportation, leadership and government, it fell to such depths due to its moral and spiritual depravity.

Gladiator was the motion picture of the year in 2000, winning five Oscars including Best Picture and Best Actor. Russell Crowe shines in his breakout performance as Maximus, the unlikely hero who was robbed of his name and his honor, whose wife and son were murdered, and who became the lowly property of slave owners. Yet against all odds, Maximus fights back from this humble place not only to gain vengeance against his enemies, but also to stem the rising tide of inhumane depravity in the Roman Empire.

Though the movie begins with Maxiumus as the commander of the armies of the north, general of the Felix legions, and loyal servant of the true emperor, Marcus Aurelius, he was treated by the emperor more as a son than a soldier. The emperor Aurelius is then viciously betrayed and killed by his own son, Commodus, who goes on to unjustly seize the throne. Out of jealousy, he does everything within his power to destroy the life of Maximus. Though forced into slavery, Maximus' skills as a superior warrior elevate him through the ranks and put him center stage in the massive, roaring Roman Colosseum. In a most dramatic scene, the gladiator sways the entire Roman mob as he almost single-hand-edly defeats all of the Roman trickery on the Colosseum floor and knocks off all of Rome's best soldiers. As the crowd is cheering for the unknown gladiator, Emperor Commodus climbs down from the elevated stands and walks onto the dirt floor of the Colosseum, seeking an audience with the gladiator. The emperor wants to know his name. After a moment of hesitation, the anonymous gladiator turns to face his enemy and courageously says, "My name is Maximus Decimus Meridius."

The testosterone level of every guy in the theater sky-rockets. What makes this scene most remarkable is that the gladiator with the least authority ends up having the greatest influence. He may have been one of the least known men in Rome, but he knew himself. Emperor Commodus, on the other hand (arguably the best known person in Rome) did not know his own true identity and, therefore, forfeited his influence. The face-off between these two iconic legends is what brought this movie to epic proportions and has made it perhaps the most popular "guy" movie of all time. At least for that moment, Maximus not only regained his own honor but also restored a level of decency and temporarily put an end to the barbaric violence, corruption and self-destruction of the Roman Colosseum and the Roman Empire.

When Christ stepped into our world, He, too, was unjustly treated by a barbaric culture. He endured injustice, was sold into slavery and treated like an animal, yet He never lost sight of His true identity. Against all odds, He single-handedly took on our evils, violence, corruption and addiction to self destruction. He stood in the authority of His own true identity to gain healing and redemption for us. Following His resurrection and ascension, it is said of Christ, "You have put all things under his feet,"[5] and again "The LORD says to my Lord: / 'Sit at my right hand, / until I make your enemies your footstool.'"[6]

Each of us has run from our God-given dominion. But even though we have rebelled against our allegiance to Him, God the Father offers to restore our authority in Christ. He invites us to walk under Christ's authority so that He can restore our authority. This restored authority is pictured by Isaiah, the prophet: "How beautiful upon the mountains / are the feet of him who brings good news."[7] When we walk in our restored authority, we will go places we never dreamed possible.

It is interesting that when Satan tempted Jesus, he took Him up to a high mountain, showed Him the kingdoms of the world and said to Him, "All these I will give you, if you will fall down and worship me."[8] This was a conflict of dominion and territory that challenged Christ's authority. If Christ had submitted to this temptation and bowed down to Satan at the beginning of His ministry, He would have relinquished His authority to the Enemy. Since He resisted the Enemy and instead chose to relinquish His authority in obedience to the Father on the cross, He defeated Satan and regained all His rightful authority for Himself—and for you and me as well. It is no wonder that, prior to His crucifixion, Jesus linked together His own death and Satan's defeat. In one sentence He said, "Now is the judgment of this world; now will the ruler of this world be cast out."[9] In the next sentence He said, regarding His death on the cross, "And I, when I am lifted up from the earth, will draw all people to myself."[10]

One of the most grotesque medical realities of crucifixion is its effect on the person's lungs. When crucifixion takes its toll and weakens the entire body, the lungs begin to fight for every breath. Because of the contortion of the body leaning awkwardly forward and the tetanus fever that causes the lungs to fill with fluid, the diaphragm is overtaxed. In order to draw breath, the upper thighs need to thrust the legs straight out to take the weight of the body off the arms and shoulders, giving room in the chest cavity to draw in new oxygen. The weight of the body is then placed on the heel, which is firmly riveted against the cross. For the last hours of life, Jesus repetitively pressed against His heel to lift His body in order to survive. Up, down, breathe; up, down, breathe—like a pile driver, Jesus drove His heel harder and harder against the supporting nail. Every upward movement of His body corresponded to a downward thrust against the weight of His heel, signifying both the bruising and rebruising of His heel and also the crushing and recrushing of the serpent's head. Truly Christ crushed evil and the Evil One under His feet.

The apostle Paul accurately described both the humiliation and the redemption of Jesus.

Christ Jesus, . . . though he was in the form of God, did not count equality with God a thing to be grasped, but emptied himself, by taking the form of a servant, being born in the likeness of men. And being found in human form, he humbled himself by becoming obedient to the point of death, even death on a cross. Therefore God has highly exalted him and bestowed on him the name that is above every name, so that at the name of Jesus every knee should bow, in heaven and on earth and under the earth, and every tongue confess that Jesus Christ is Lord, to the glory of God the Father.[11]

A TWENTY-FIRST-CENTURY HEALING

Sitting in a café in Jerusalem, Ibrahim overheard a Muslim man next to him in a heated argument on his mobile phone. Due to the high volume and intensity of the conversation, Ibrahim couldn't help but take notice of the conversation.

As the man hung up, he sighed out loud, "O, how I hate the Jews!" Ibrahim looked in the man's direction, smiled and nodded empathetically. "May I introduce myself?" As the man gave him eye contact, Ibrahim added, "I can understand how you feel toward the Jews; I have an unusual story that I think you will appreciate." The man seemed intrigued, so Ibrahim continued.

"My family members have also been victims of great injustice, first from the Jews and then from the Muslims. Here in Israel we owned a large plot of land in a large town. Not just any land—it was prime real estate. Then, when we as Arabs were evicted from Palestine in 1948, we were forced to give our property to the new state of Israel. As you know, the United Nations gave us no financial compensation whatsoever. We went from being wealthy people to homeless refugees, so we fled to a neighboring Arab country."

The young Muslim man listened with wide-eyed interest as Ibrahim continued. "My father never told us how much the land was worth, because he knew it would make us even more bitter. When we became refugees, we had absolutely nothing, but this was only the beginning. In Israel, we had lost everything to the Jews, but now things were even worse. We became victims of great injustice, oppression and racism, living as Christian people in a predominately Muslim country. It was extremely painful.

"I worked hard in school and became first in my class; I knew that education was my only way out. When the United States created a program for exchange students, I was number one on the list. At sixteen years old, I applied for the program to become an exchange student in the United States. It promised me a college education in a country where I would be respected. As the star student at the top of my class, I was counting on this award. My principal even guaranteed me that my position was locked up. He assured me that my grades were far better than anyone else's and my references were sterling. There was no way anyone was going to cut in line in front of me this time—or so I thought!"

The Muslim man inquired, "Okay, so what happened?"

Ibrahim concluded his story. "When it came time to award the prize and the winning student was announced—his name was Muhammad. I was furious! A Muslim had beaten me, even though I was academically better and everyone agreed that I was unquestionably more qualified. It was like a dagger in my heart. I was devastated. Anger and hatred erupted within me like a volcano. I didn't want anything to do with Muslims. I had been the victim of oppression, racial profiling and injustice."

"I get the picture," the Muslim man nodded.

Ibrahim then told his new friend, "A few years later, I met a man who had lived here in Israel—His name is Jesus. Perhaps you have heard of Him?" Ibrahim waited for a smile from his new friend and got one.

"I learned that Christ had suffered severely and unjustly in order to forgive me for far worse crimes than anyone had ever committed against me—I was overwhelmed. Jesus' love changed me. I was compelled to forgive those who had mistreated me.

"Then my major breakthrough came. On May 10, I was baptized in the Holy Spirit. The Holy Spirit came in and cleansed me with fire. I was filled to overflowing with the love of God, and that love became like a river in my soul. I knew at once that not only was I forgiven, but I was now in a forgiving river. Forgiveness poured out of my life like a river that had overflowed its banks. My tank of forgiveness was filled to overflowing; I forgave the Jews who had taken our land when I was a child, and I forgave the Muslims who had seemingly taken away my future. Think of it—the same day that I was baptized in the Holy Spirit, I forgave the Jews and the Muslims, all at the same time.

"That same day, I was also called by God to spend the rest of my life serving both Jews and Muslims. He called me to love everyone—everyone on earth—and I have spent my entire life from that moment on, serving, loving and forgiving both Jews and Muslims alike. Why God would choose a Palestinian Arab Christian and send him on a mission to both Jews and Muslims, I can't tell you. It took a miracle, and that's what it is!"

The man at the café table looked at Ibrahim with eyes wide and said, "I have never heard a story like this."

"I have never known a Savior like this!" Ibrahim added without hesitation, "and I guarantee you that everything I am telling you right now is absolutely true. It is the miracle of being overtaken by the love of Christ."

Every year Ibrahim Ayoub (not his real name)[12] talks with tens of thousands of people about the healing wounds of Jesus—people from Christian, Muslim and

Jewish backgrounds. Because he has come under the authority of Christ, he walks in authority. Today, he is considered by many to be one of the most influential Christians in the Middle East. Ibrahim told me that after his dad died in 1988, he and his family learned that the piece of property taken from them was worth several million dollars. But Ibrahim then explained, "That's nothing compared to the size of my moral and spiritual debt that Jesus paid for me. He didn't just forgive me; His wounds healed me."

God made you to walk in authority, but the only way for you to regain your authority is to come under God's authority. And the only way to come under God's authority is to give Him control of your life.

The thought of relinquishing control to someone else is intimidating. In order to deal effectively with your fears, you need something working inside you that is stronger than your fears. What could be stronger than your fears? The apostle John tells us, "There is no fear in love, but perfect love casts out fear. For fear has to do with punishment, and whoever fears has not been perfected in love."[13] Jesus' pierced feet should be enough to prove to you once and for all just how much He loves you. Once the love of Christ overpowers your fear of losing control and casts that fear from you, you will then be in a place to relinquish the control of your life to Him. You can trust Him.

8

THE SIDE OF JESUS
Redeeming Our Hearts

One of the soldiers pierced his side with a spear, and at once there came out blood and water.

John 19: 34

Most premed students, hospital orderlies and RNs have a defining moment during their early training when they experience firsthand that all life is in the blood.

A patient is placed on a gurney and rushed into the emergency room. All color has drained from the person's skin, causing the individual to look more like a manne-quin than a person. The brain is oxygen starved, the lips are pale, and the skin looks like dry clay. It is virtually impossible to get a pulse. Then a unit of blood arrives. It's buckled on a high metal rod, and the tube running from it is inserted by needle into the person's vein. The bottle empties quickly. Another unit of blood is added, then another. Then the miracle occurs. The first pink appears in the cheeks. The lips darken. Then the patient draws a first spasmodic breath. The person's eyes flutter. The patient squints as if seeing light for the first time. Soon the person becomes conscious—the dead awakens. Life has entered back into the body. It's nothing short of resurrection.

This illustrates a basic medical principle: Life is literally in the blood. What happens on hospital gurneys virtually every day is a vivid, accurate picture of a parallel spiritual reality. In Jesus' seventh wound, the life truly is in the blood—in this case, the blood of Christ. Too many people today have tragically and unnecessarily distanced themselves from the blood of Christ because they think it's primitive or archaic. If there has ever been a generation in history that should understand that life is in the blood, it is ours.

Medical doctors tell us that there are between five and six liters of blood in the human body, making up 7 percent of a person's body mass. Nearly this much blood would have flowed from Jesus' body with His seventh wound. It is hard to fathom that the first wound, which began in Jesus' sweat glands in the garden, would lead to six other wounds from which Jesus would bleed and *which would eventually drain every drop of blood from His vascular network.*

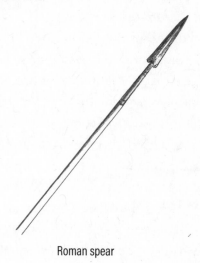

Roman spear

The seventh and final wound of Christ is the deepest wound of all. The metal tip of the Roman spear that was thrust into Jesus' body was no less than twelve inches long. When the spear tip penetrated Jesus' side, slid up under His rib cage and punctured the pericardium sac, it actually went all the way into Jesus' chest and pierced His heart. This wound of Christ, known historically as the wound to His side, is actually the wound to Jesus' heart. The heart is the core of who we are. It is the seat of our affections; the place of our identity; the space from which we sift out good from evil, right from wrong and safety from threat. If we damage the heart, we damage the person—the self-worth, security and significance. Heart wounds run deep.

Perhaps nothing reveals people's heart wounds today more vividly than the fact that we are rapidly becoming a generation riddled with anxiety disorders and chronic fear. A research study was recently conducted of twenty-two hundred eleven-year-olds. The findings were shocking. Virtually every one of these sixth-grade students was gripped by an overwhelming sense of fear. Two out of every four feared going to sleep. Half of them feared going outside. The study concluded that this increase of fear among middle school students is due partially to violent television and brutal video games. Psychologists say that fear keeps them in business. Charles Mayo, founder of the Mayo Clinic, said, "I've never known a man who died from overwork, but I've known many who have died from doubt."[1]

CHRIST'S SURRENDER

This seventh and final wound of Christ corresponds to His surrender of the heart. The spear thrust into Jesus' physical heart represents a deeper inward wound that He experienced in His heart of hearts—the wounds of rejection, fear and insignificance. Did Christ feel rejection? Jesus had known nothing but acceptance from His Father; yet when He received this physical heart wound, He experienced the heart wound of rejection in a number of ways. At the start of His life, His stepfather, Joseph, wanted to reject Him and put Him away quietly. Now, in the final hours of His life, Jesus had been betrayed by a close associate and utterly forsaken by His colleagues. He tragically tasted the bitterness of rejection and could identify with the words of Isaiah the prophet, "He was despised and rejected by men, / a man of sorrows and acquainted with grief / . . . as one from whom men hide their faces."[2]

Did Christ feel fear and insecurity? Christ had known nothing but security with God; yet at the end of His life, He experienced all our vulnerabilities and threats. On the last night of His life, from the garden of Gethsemane, remember His hematidrosis or blood sweats, when he cried out to God in deepest agony?[3] We are told that He "offered up prayers and supplications, with loud cries and tears, to him who was able to save him from death."[4] It was said of Him that He was poured out like water and that His heart melted like wax in His chest.[5]

Did Christ feel insignificance? He had lived with a compelling sense of self-worth and significance; yet prior to His death, he was abandoned and forsaken. Christ had experienced nothing but deep intimacy with the

Father; and He even enjoyed the honors of being worshiped by angels, we are told. But in the darkest hour on the cross, only moments before His seventh wound was inflicted, Jesus felt the chilling sting of rejection and cried out in absolute anguish, "My God, my God, why have you forsaken me?"[6] He had been utterly abandoned and He knew it.

Jesus would never have subjected His soul to such heart wounds without good cause. His plan was to be able to provide us with both healing and immunity to our own heart diseases. He knew that He needed to receive in Himself these toxic soul sicknesses in order to be qualified to bring us healing by blood transfusion.

Dr. Claude Barlow was a medical doctor who invested a lifetime in humanitarian work in China and Africa fighting tropical diseases. He received his MD degree from Northwestern in 1906 and later received an additional degree in tropical diseases from Johns Hopkins University in 1929. In addition to English, he was able to speak Arabic, German and Chinese. In 1948, he received a certificate of merit from President Harry Truman. The *Grand Rapids Press* published an article documenting a most extraordinary method used by Dr. Barlow to find a cure for the horrible tropical disease known as snail fever, or schistosomiasis. The *Grand Rapids Press* referred to it as, "the widest spread and most crippling disease known to the world . . . in the wet tropical climates of the Orient, Africa, and South America." After discovering this incurable disease and hitting every roadblock for finding a cure, he devised a plan. He secretly ingested the Chinese parasites into his own body, admitted himself into Johns Hopkins and into the care of the same medical doctors from whom he had received his medical degree years earlier. He spent day and night in the laboratory as they treated his illness.

"Did you tell any of the other missionaries what you have done," the doctors questioned.

"No," he answered.

"Did you tell your wife," they asked.

"No, I did not tell anyone; I boarded a ship and came to America," Barlow replied.

During the several months at sea, the parasites had plenty of time to multiply. But Dr. Barlow entrusted himself into the care of the physicians; and, in the process they were able not only to cure Barlow, but also to find a cure for the tropical disease. That cure has now saved hundreds of thousands of lives around the world and all but eradicated snail fever.[7]

In the same way, Christ knew humankind needed the cure for our incurable heart diseases of fear, rejection and insignificance—so He devised a plan. He Himself drank these heart diseases for all humanity on the cross.

He then entrusted Himself to His Father God to find the cure—and God did! This is the story of redemption. This is the miracle of Christ and His blood.

After every last drop drained from Christ's heart, He died. He was buried, and three days later He rose from the dead. There is now a cure for all our heart diseases.

OUR HEALING

This seventh and final wound of Jesus corresponds with our deepest wounds of all—the wounds to the heart. In reference to our heart diseases, the Bible says, "The heart is deceitful above all things, and desperately sick."[8] Jesus Himself said, "From within, out of the heart of man, come evil thoughts, sexual immorality, theft, murder, adultery, coveting, wickedness, deceit, sensuality, envy, slander, pride, foolishness. All these evil things come from within, and they defile a person."[9] Humankind has heart problems, we might as well admit it. With human heart wounds that run this deep, it is no wonder that Christ's pericardium was pierced. His heart was wounded to heal our heart wounds. You and I need a radical and thorough blood transfusion.

Have you felt the heart wound of rejection? The blood of Christ can deliver you from the spirit of rejection and replace it with unconditional acceptance.

God promised us, "Since, therefore, we have now been justified by his blood, much more shall we be saved by him from the wrath of God."[10] Just think of it—you can be fully justified and fully accepted because of the blood of Christ. Your heart wound of rejection can now be healed with the acceptance of Christ. Have you felt the plaguing fears of insecurity? The blood of Christ can heal your fears, anxieties, and insecurities and impart to you safety and security. God promises us, "God was pleased...through him [Christ] to reconcile to himself all things, . . . making peace by the blood of his cross."[11] When you are reconciled to God, you will have peace with Him and within yourself. God's perfect love for you will drive out all fear from your heart.[12] You too, can be safe and secure in Christ.

Have you felt the wound to your self-worth and the gnawing emptiness of insignificance? The blood of Christ can heal your heart from these feelings and re-place them with a profound awareness of your own sig-nificance. You are significant to God when you are in Christ. The Bible says of Christ, "You were slain, and by your blood you ransomed people for God from every tribe and language and people and nation."[13]

What a picture! What a promise! What a reality! Sometimes we think that world religions are geograph-ically regional—for example, we believe that Islam is for Middle Easterners, Hinduism is for Indians and Buddhism is for Southeast Asians. But this thinking is myopic and misses the point. The blood of Christ transcends geography and redeems people from every tribe and language and nation. The wounds of Christ are for the healing of the nations. Directly prior to receiving His seventh wound, Jesus spoke the epic words, "It is finished." The historic account documents it this way: "When Jesus had received the sour wine, he said, 'It is finished,' and he bowed his head and gave up his spirit."[14] The actual word that Jesus spoke in Aramaic was *tetelestai.* It was a commercial word that technically meant "paid in full." When you go to Home Depot and purchase a large quantity of lumber, you then drive your pickup truck to the loading dock, show them the invoice marked "paid in full" and pick up your supplies.

Similarly, Jesus, on the cross, paid the astronomical moral and spiritual debt that we had accumulated—all our boneheaded choices, stubborn rebellion, selfish ambition, twisted pride, guilt and shame—and in one moment, with the shedding of His own blood, paid the entire debt in full. Ultimately, the love relationship Christ is seeking with you is not simply for a time but for eternity. Jesus wants to establish an authentic love relationship with you today that will literally last forever.

That's why we call Him Savior. That is why His seven wounds bring unexpected healing to skeptics, cynics and seekers alike.

A TWENTY-FIRST-CENTURY HEALING

The phone rang. From the sound of his son's voice, Don knew instantly that something was badly wrong. The news that he would receive in the next five minutes would change Don's life forever.

"Dad, you have been trying for years to get to the bottom of your daughter's problems—her emotional wounds, eating disorders and depression. Dad, I never wanted to tell you this, because I knew the news would be crushing. But I need to tell you. Your daughter was sexually abused as a child. She was the victim of a horrible crime. And Dad, I am so sorry to have to tell you who the predator was." After a long pause, Don's son gave him the chilling news: "Dad, it was Grandpa. Your father molested your daughter."

The news was overwhelming. Devastating. It left Don with more questions than answers. He was limp. He immediately got into his car and drove four hours to confront his father face to face, which only confirmed his worst nightmare. But this was only the beginning. Months later he learned the equally devastating news that his father had molested not only his daughter but two of his sons as well.

Don was well aware that as a Christian, he was required to forgive his father, and he did so in his mind; but he never forgave his father from the heart. It wasn't until he was standing in front of an audience talking about the importance of forgiveness that God said to him, "What are you saying? How can you preach to others what you have never done from your own heart? You have not yet forgiven your father. Not really!"

Those words literally knocked Don to his knees. There he was, in front of a large group of people, and all he could do was kneel down and sob uncontrollably. He was shaking, sobbing, reeling under the conviction of God to his own heart.

While kneeling at the front of the auditorium, Don did business with God. He realized God's patience with him through the years and the forgiveness that God had shown him through the cross of Christ. The internal impact of the enormity of God's love for Don seemed to shift something inside his heart. Eventually, when he gathered himself and rose to his feet, he was able to explain to his listeners what had just taken place and the mountain of resentment, bitterness and unforgiveness that had just been drained from his heart. Now, years later, Don has truly forgiven his father from the heart. The poison of unforgiveness has drained from his system, and he is free—free indeed! All this happened because of the loving wounds of Christ, particularly the wound to Jesus' heart, which replaced the resentment and bitterness left inside Don's. Don now has an extensive healing, forgiveness and deliverance ministry around the world.

If you have been walking down your own path of pain, I want to introduce you to the One who walked it before you—Christ, the wounded healer. He took up your sickness and carried your sorrows. And the best part of all is that He loves you.

The single blockage that causes most heart problems is unforgiveness. Who is it in your life that you need to forgive—your ex, your abusive stepdad, your overbearing mother, your mother-in-law, the person you thought was your best friend? If you want God to heal your heart, you may need to allow Him to deliver you from unforgiveness. Forgiveness is saying to someone, "I give up my right to hurt you even though you hurt me." We live in a world that thinks the greatest power on earth is unforgiveness, resentment and retaliation. Wrong. The greatest power on earth is forgiveness.

As you may recall, in the preface we defined ground zero as "the point on the earth's surface above and below an exploding nuclear bomb." We then made the observation that the cross of Christ marks ground zero for all humanity throughout history. Above the cross, a forgiveness revolution began, as Father God is now able to justly forgive our sins because of Christ's sacrificial life payment—because of Christ's blood. Jesus expressed the impact of this nuclear-sized sacrifice when He declared with His final words, "It is finished."[15]

Beneath the cross, a similar forgiveness revolution began. Those who receive Christ's forgiving blood sacrifice are now able to extend forgiveness to others. Christ expressed this impact of the forgiveness revolution beneath the cross when he declared the epic words, "Father, forgive them, for they know not what they do."[16] Once the nuclear explosion of God's forgiveness is released into your heart, your life will change. You can then turn to those who have hurt and offended you and express the same kind of forgiveness toward them. The cross is the headwaters of the forgiveness revolution.

The reason Christ wants to heal your heart is because He wants a love relationship with you.

The seven wounds of Christ, particularly His heart wound, should convince you that God wants more from you than merely a superficial relationship; He wants to go deep with you. You do not need to keep yourself at arm's length from God—He loves you! You can trust Him. If the seven wounds say anything to you, on behalf of God they say, "I love you, I have given all for you, I am ready to heal you, and you can trust me."

No matter where you are with God, Christ invites you to go deeper with Him today. He is ready to heal your heart.

SMALL GROUP STUDY GUIDE

The following application questions have been prepared for your benefit. They correspond to each chapter in this book. They are designed to help create stimulating discussion as you review the content and make personal application.

WEEK 1:
WALK WITH ME!
His Wounds, Our Healing

1. Has anyone in your group been to Jerusalem? Did you walk down the Via Dolorosa? What was your experience?

2. Which of the three sites in this chapter struck the deepest chord in you—the hill of the skull, the whipping stone or the garden of Gethsemane?

3. The author gives three suggestions as you read through this book: Have hope, get real, go deep. Which of these suggestions struck a chord in you and why?

4. What is meant by the statement "Jesus' wounds are our wounds"?

5. What is meant by this statement: "This short book is as much about self-discovery as historic discovery"?

6. Using your own words, how would you describe Michael, the man who came to the Church of the Sepulcher as a last ditch effort? Is there anything about him with which you can identify?

WEEK 2:
THE SWEAT OF JESUS
Reshaping our Wills

1. It's hard to imagine the level of stress to which Jesus was subject when He experienced hematidrosis. What factors contributed to this level of anxiety?

2. Why do you think Jesus loved Gethsemane?

3. What is the meaning of the name "Gethsemane"? What is the significance of this name in reference to Christ's passion?

4. In Gethsemane, Jesus obviously submitted His will to God. He surrendered His will in order to heal our wounded wills. In what ways are our wills wounded? Be specific.

5. How does the garden of Gethsemane reverse the curse from the garden of Eden?

6. In your own words, describe the angry Arab youth, Jack. What change did Jesus bring to his life?

7. Why is it frightening and intimidating to relinquish control to God? Why is this surrender so important in order for us to have a love relationship with God?

WEEK 3:
THE FACE OF JESUS

Recovering Our Identity

1. When you read the medical account at the beginning of this chapter describing how we are actually washed internally by the blood, what were your thoughts?

2. Let's review. Make a list of all the specific ways in which Jesus' face was abused.

3. What does the face represent that helps us understand exactly what Jesus surrendered?

4. Do you agree that most people have issues with their own self-worth? Why do you say so?

5. What unusual issues did Nick Vujicic have to deal with? What pain did he feel? How did God's love make a difference in his life?

6. This is a very personal question, but have you ever been the victim of bullying? Have you ever felt loneliness, depression, insecurity or self-hatred? If so, how do you respond to Jesus' face wounds?

WEEK 4:
THE BACK OF JESUS
Regaining Our Health

1. The wounds to Jesus' back are by far the most gruesome of all His wounds. When you read the account of flagellation at the beginning of the chapter, how did it make you feel?

2. When Jesus surrendered His back, He was obviously surrendering His physical well-being. Why would He do such a thing?

3. Have someone in the group read aloud Isaiah 53:3–6. While these words were written hundreds of years before Jesus was born, how do they closely resemble what Jesus experienced?

4. In your own words, how would you explain the difference between true divine healing and other approaches to healing?

5. What was your response to the healing of Susana's eyes? What do you think about her healing?

6. Have you ever experienced divine healing? Tell your story.

7. Respond to this statement: "We don't promise you healing, but we promise you Jesus. He loves you, and He is a healer."

WEEK 5:
THE HEAD OF JESUS
Reclaiming Our Dignity

1. When the Roman soldiers put the crown on Jesus' head, what were they intending to express?

2. What do you imagine Jesus felt when He was being ruthlessly mocked?

3. Since a crown is normally a symbol of honor, why was it appropriate that Jesus should wear the mocking crown of thorns?

4. When Christ wore the crown of thorns, what was He surrendering?

5. Let's be honest—how have you experienced damaged self-worth? Be specific.

6. When you read Christy's story, with what could you identify? Be specific.

7. What did Jesus restore in Christy's life?

WEEK 6:
THE HANDS OF JESUS
Reestablishing Our Productivity

1. The actual act of crucifixion began by driving nails through Jesus' wrists. When this took place, what did Jesus obviously surrender?

2. Before this wound was inflicted, what specific ways had Jesus used His hands?

3. In what way did the act of disobedience in the garden of Eden affect the productivity of humankind?

4. What is the connection between unproductivity and unfulfillment?

5. What do we learn from the author's young son who picked up a carving knife around the blade?

6. What crisis did Al Hartley face? Can any of you identify with Al?

7. What did Jesus restore to Al Hartley?

WEEK 7:
THE FEET OF JESUS
Restoring Our Authority

1. What can we learn about ourselves from the story about blood transfusion at the beginning of the chapter? What can we learn about Jesus?

2. When Jesus was wounded in His feet, what did He surrender?

3. What is significant about the statement God made in the garden of Eden, "I will put enmity between you and the woman, / and between your offspring and her offspring; / he shall bruise your head, / and you shall bruise his heel"?[1]

4. What important principle is illustrated in the famous movie *Gladiator*? What do we learn from Maximus that reminds us of Jesus?

5. What hardship did Ibrahim experience? What important lesson did Ibrahim communicate to his new Muslim friend?

WEEK 8:
THE SIDE OF JESUS
Redeeming Our Hearts

1. When you read the medical explanation at the beginning of this chapter showing that life is in the blood, what did you learn about the blood of Christ?

2. This final wound to the heart illustrates how Jesus wants to heal us at the core of who we are. What does this statement mean: "Heart wounds run deep"?

3. Why is the cross called "ground zero"? In what way is this an appropriate word picture?

4. Dr. Claude Barlow voluntarily drank vials full of disease in order to submit himself to medical doctors and find a cure. What does this story illustrate? How did Jesus do something similar?

5. Of the three specific heart wounds identified in this chapter—rejection, insecurity and insignificance— which ones have you experienced in your own life? Let's get personal.

6. Specifically, how can Jesus heal our heart wounds? How does He heal our insecurity? Our fears? Our sense of insignificance?

7. Describe what Don would have felt when he learned how his own father had victimized his children. What did Jesus do for Don?

8. Why is forgiveness so essential between us and God? Between us and other people in our lives?

NOTES

PREFACE

1. C.S. Lewis, *The Problem of Pain* (San Francisco: HarperOne, 1996), 91.

2. Isaiah 53:4–5, NIV.

3. First Corinthians 1:23.

4. Revelation 12:11, NIV.

CHAPTER 1: WALK WITH ME!

1. The Via Dolorosa is the path that Jesus walked on the way to His crucifixion. The original path began in Gethsemane. The current route, however, begins at the Antonia Fortress just inside the Lion's Gate; it was established in the eighteenth century and is marked by fourteen stations of the cross (nine on the path and five inside the Church of the Holy Sepulcher):

   Station 1: Jesus is condemned to death in front of Pilate (this is where Jesus receives wounds two and three, to His face and His back). Station 2: Jesus carries His cross. Station 3: Jesus falls for the first time. Station 4: Jesus meets His mother. Station 5: Simon of Cyrene helps Jesus carry the cross. Station 6: A woman wipes Jesus' face.

Station 7: Jesus falls a second time. Station 8: Jesus meets the women of Jerusalem. Station 9: Jesus falls a third time. Station 10: Jesus is stripped of His outer clothes (this is where Jesus receives wound four, to His head). Station 11: Jesus is crucified (this is where Jesus receives wounds five and six, to His hands and feet). Station 12: Jesus dies on the cross (this is where Jesus receives His seventh and final wound, to His side). Station 13: Jesus is prepared for burial. Station 14: Jesus is laid in a tomb, from which He will arise three days later.

2. Isaiah 53:4–6.

3. John 3:16, NIV.

CHAPTER 2: THE SWEAT OF JESUS

1. John 10:17–18.

2. John 19:11.

3. Matthew 26:53.

4. Matthew 26:42.

5. Luke 22:42.

6. Luke 22:44.

7. Isaiah 61:1.

8. Luke 4:21.

9. "Michael Phelps Workout and Diet," *Muscle Prodigy*, October 29, 2016, https://www.muscleprodigy.com/michael-phelps-workout-and-diet.

10. Genesis 2:16–17.

11. Romans 7:15.

12. Philippians 2:13.

13. First John 4:10.

CHAPTER 3: THE FACE OF JESUS

1. Ibid.

2. Matthew 27:30.

3. Mark 14:65.

4. Mark 15:19.

5. Luke 22:63.

6. John 18:22.

7. John 19:3.

8. Isaiah 50:6.

9. Isaiah 53:3.

10. Psalm 27:4, NIV.

11. Philippians 2:5–7.

12. "Dove Real Beauty Sketches," *Dove US,* September 23, 2015, https://www.dove.com/us/en/stories/campaigns/real-beauty-sketches.html.

13. Genesis 1:26.

14. Psalm 139:13–14.

15. Nick Vujicic, *Life Without Limits: Inspiration for a Ridiculously Good Life* (Colorado Springs: WaterBrook, 2012), viii.

16. First John 4:19.

CHAPTER 4: THE BACK OF JESUS

1. See Matthew 27:26; Mark 15:15.

2. Isaiah 50:6.

3. Isaiah 53:4, NIV.

4. Isaiah 53:5.

5. Matthew 8:16–17.

6. First Corinthians 6:13.

7. Romans 8:11.

CHAPTER 5: THE HEAD OF JESUS

1. See John 19:1–2.

2. See Matthew 27:26–31; Mark 15:16–20.

3. John Hutton Balfour, *The Plants of the Bible* (London: T. Nelson and Sons, 1885), 128.

4. Genesis 3:17–18.

5. See Luke 23:53. The shroud was the primary large fabric wrapped around Christ's body following crucifixion. It was one of two or more cloths used (see John 20:6–7).

6. John 19:5.

7. Psalm 3:3.

8. See Revelation 21:1.

9. Romans 8:23.

10. Colossians 1:15–20.

11. Romans 5:8.

CHAPTER 6: THE HANDS OF JESUS

1. John 17:4.

2. John 4:34.

3. John 19:30.

4. John 10:17–18.

5. Matthew 11:28.

6. Mark 14:22.

7. Genesis 1:28.

8. Genesis 2:16–17.

CHAPTER 7: THE FEET OF JESUS

1. Ibid.

2. Psalm 22:16.

3. Psalm 24:1, NIV.

4. Hebrew 2:6–8; see also Romans 16:20.

5. Psalm 8:6.

6. Psalm 110:1.

7. Isaiah 52:7.

8. Matthew 4:9.

9. John 12:31.

10. John 12:32.

11. Philippians 2:5–11.

12. This is the only name change in the entire book. In order to maintain the integrity of the story as well as protect the safety of my friend, the change was essential.

13. First John 4:18.

CHAPTER 8: THE SIDE OF JESUS

1. Zig Ziglar, "Zig on . . . Worry," *Christian Post*, December 3, 2009, accessed December 15, 2016, http://www.christianpost.com/news/42108/.

2. Isaiah 53:3.

3. See Luke 22:44.

4. Hebrews 5:7.

5. See Psalm 22:14.

6. Matthew 27:46.

7. Holmes, Susan, and John F. Barlow, "Dr. Claude Heman Barlow October 13, 1876 - October 08, 1969," *Dr. Claude Heman Barlow*, accessed May 29, 2017, http://www.barlowgenealogy.com/Edmund-ofMalden/DrCHBarlow1.html

8. Jeremiah 17:9.

9. Mark 7:21–23.

10. Romans 5:9.

11. Colossians 1:19–20.

12. See First John 4:18.

13. Revelation 5:9.

14. John 19:30.

15. Ibid.

16. Luke 23:34.

SMALL GROUP STUDY GUIDE

1. Genesis 3:15.

To know more about the remarkable story of the founding
of CLC International we encourage you to read:

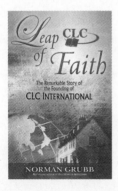

LEAP OF FAITH

Norman Grubb

Paperback

Size 5¹/₄ x 8, Pages 248

ISBN: 978-0-87508-650-7

ISBN (*e-book*): 978-1-61958-055-8

GOD ON FIRE

Fred A. Hartley III

As believers, we are more alive in the middle of God's white-hot presence than anywhere else on earth. The history of revival is often studied from man's perspective; what we do to encounter God. *God on Fire* explores what God does to encounter us.

Paperback
Size 5 ¼ x 8, Pages 206
ISBN 978-1-61958-012-1
ISBN (*e-book*) 978-1-61958-066-4

"Your work, brethren, is to set your church on fire somehow."
–Charles H. Spurgeon

CHURCH
ON
FIRE

A 31-Day Adventure to Welcome
the Manifest Presence of Christ

Fred A. Hartley, III

CHURCH ON FIRE

Fred A. Hartley III

Church on Fire by Fred Hartley is a study that takes churches on a thirty-one-day journey toward the manifest presence of Christ in the life of the Body. Each week includes five chapters, which require reflection, study, and prayer as well a section for pastors and discussion questions for small groups.

Paperback
Size 6 x 9, Pages 167
ISBN: 978-1-61958-180-7
ISBN (*e-book*): 978-1-61958-181-4

"El trabajo de ustedes, hermanos, es de alguna manera encender el fuego en su iglesia." —Charles H. Spurgeon

IGLESIA EN FUEGO

Una aventura de 31 días para la bienvenida a la presencia manifiesta de Cristo

Fred A. Hartley, III

IGLESIA EN FUEGO

Fred A. Hartley III

Iglesia en Fuego es lo que ocurre cuando Cristo llega a la iglesia. Es un libro práctico, relacional, misional y listo para poner por obra. Por qué conformarse con sólo mantener la maquinaria de la iglesia en movimiento, ¡cuando Dios está esperando para establecer su Iglesia en el fuego!

Paperback
Size 5 ⁷⁄₁₆ x 8 ⅜₆ , Pages 277
ISBN: 978-1-61958-213-2
ISBN (*e-book*): 978-1-61958-214-9